The End of Aesthetics and the
Philosophy of Violence

The Magical Language

Israel Against Iran

The War That Would Change the World

Iran's nuclear ambition.

There are no final solutions,only a never ending game of politics among states and groups of common interest.The cohesion of the fighitng groups derive from various parameters.

Indifference is the modern fascism.

Discriminations that international customary law cannot change.Fake ethics and hypocrisy of the elits.

Memory of glass.The polemics of federalization.The forever sadness of devilish tomorrows.What is hate?He asked anxiously.What is the yesterday graveyard and stone emblem?The white sculpture,the white fiscal policies of dead tompstones.The coffins where black as the ghosts returned back.Words come as a flow inside a dark river.The upheaval of meanings drive the crash of idealistic superforms.The river of words colides with the void of forms and images of past perfection that will never repeat themselves.The idealism and classicist mind of the golden age has been abandoned has given its place to the useless necessity of violent measures.They are hard fugitives of underground reality spectacles.Which have passed and won the new forms of perfectness,the foolish,feasible ,universal,earth of roots.And his

name meant,because forever worthy
he is plus the previous
quality.Magical alphabets flowed
from the top of the headless chickens
but not meant to be offensive just
symbolically perplexed.The
bewildermentof thoughts can forever
pass as innosence and white figures
of passive death.Where are my
senses when I will exist as a spirit of
the undead as an aethereal being of
nothingness.As a corpse of the just
married couple.The beauty of the
weak can never prove its
existence,only when it stops to exist
we notice the difference.Beauty of
forms is a forgotten principle.Today
productivity reigns as the
supreme,magical
supremacy.Fundamentalism is the
return to the roots,black from

melanine.When will my death arrive as salvation?If he was certain of post mortem existence he would end his journey and he would stop to feel,as the drugs make you numb,make you to feel nothingness and emptiness .He could observe the new beauty in necrophilia,or perhaps a return to the rules of ancient Egypt and mummification.He needed to be violent in order to stay alive.

The ugly face of decadent society.The reality of the inner nature of random mutations.The violent nature that is essential for survival.The explosion of adrenaline.

Murderers of fake voluntary dead coffins ,of dreadfull junta ,of downward streaming trends of waves.The reality shows drive the

philosophical peculiarities the dogma
of action for the future.The creation
of personal imaginary words.The
autism of the future man and the end
of autism when we participate in the
media mass democracy.If it exists in
the media it becomes a reality.The
reality of real nature is preferable to
the perfectionist aesthetics of
classical values.Practicality becomes
superior to the polemics of yesterday
formalisms.The concept of
spacetime is a formalism ,a
convention of the physicists.Time
cannot be curved unlike space or
magnetic fields.Time preexists the
creation of matter from the God
particle.Matter is a mutation of the
void or a vibration of the God
particle.

Creating strategies and tacticisms.That is the ability of the complex minds.Being the player,the gambler has mindful implications,is the symbol of leadership for space colonies.The colonizer will be a military hero,don't forget that when you think and plan your future military junta.It will bring the new values of Darwinism and algebraic formulations as dead tigers that they wanted to rape.Forgetfulness of past behavior is a prelude to future losses.Cut your losses short.An important lesson an experienced gambler carries with him.The early men could rise as relics of animal primates or spirits.The cubic brain is the strength of nootropics.Pills can create thematic parks in your brain,which is the polemics of tomorrow.The future autism is predicted by the orthodoxy of religious participation.To be a person with a legal face means to participate in the mass performances of symbolic politics.Success is judged by the ability to mimick the median and the one next to you.

 We have to feel complete with the inadequate uses of new meanings.The reprogramming of the collective mind.The eternal battle between the two opposites has historical images.When evilness becomes mainstream one more time in history since the ancient Sodom and Gommorah,the new Messiah or Antichrist will have arrived.The manihaism of yesterdays will end when the military junta takes over power.Hate me forever,said the crippled by the mines,son.I went to all the nightclubs and they all recognized me as the boss of crime as a cult figure who prevails and is a tough guy.Hate me as long as I live and I will be fed with your hatred.I will grow with your hatred.Bigger and bigger until I reach the stars.The heuristics of manipulation is a system of thoughts and rules that will give birthto the new games and horseraces.

The return of Nazism as Zionism is the two faces of the same coin,interdependent and solid like the relation between differentiation and integration.Like the night,it cannot exist without the day.The return of brutality will be vital for the rebirth of our national order and productivity.Hate me forever said the unearthly circular mind of symbolic policies ,of military exercises and festivals.It is time to stop being weak.Stop to exist without order.

The crippled Messiah of the millenium will allways mourn his losses as a super reality check of forever grim reapers.

Philosopohy is entertainment.That's the new civilization I am building.

Personal paradise and anarchy.Endless battle for survival and victory.What is Postnietzcheism.

We replace aesthetics with indulgence and the satisfaction of feelings.How ever obscure or random they may be.

The weddings will transform into funerals.Coffins will open and the undead will take power with a coup.Defencive schemes will achieve victory.The beauty of funerals will be seen by everyone,it will become mainstream.Hate is the forever illusion.We can be calm with a strange feeling of playing and taking risks like a game of poker where our lives are in stake but at the same time a sense of protection and safety is present.We come to a point where we appreciate reality through keen observation of facts.We come to realise the calm effect of taking risks.Major wars are designed like games of poker.Women choose their beloved.With a black wedding dress the undeadbride will get married in the underworld.

Mental accounting is present in the calculations of obscene facts.I want to recruit some soldiers,they will help me to make money.

Globalization brings the bankruptcy of weak nations and the downsize of the public sector in strong nations.

Latin America and the Balkans are experiment tubes for new methods of outside military intervention and control through excessive debt.A new bipolarity will arise with China in the role of the new opposing superpower.International bankers need that form of arrangement to govern the masses .In the age of globalization only they are the real winners from bankruptcies,crises and wars against terrorism.

Let's celebrate the begineng of the new age which will be similar to the old age as political regimes are cyclical.The army will play a more decisive role in the future policy making as security threats like terrorism will be more prevalent.

Strategic positioning is the adjustment of balance between strategic fit and strategic stretch.To be like the others or to change the world in order to resemble as ,that is the dilemma.If the state does not intervene what is the meaning of political behavior and choice.That is a question that will keep the philosopher'smind busy.Espescially the neoliberal mind.

Real neoliberalism should not be confused with old fashioned conservatism.Real neoliberalism is offering freedoms to the individualto create his own way of life and his own environment.The real question is if those who hold power of coercion are willing to not act in order for the other people to make their choices.Even if those choices are against Christian values or they are self-destructive.Is neoliberalism a true expansion of freedoms ase the word indicates ,or it is the hidden face of old power centers.The Russian oligarchs are the same kind of men like the American robber barons.Every new scientific and economic trend creates its own new leaders.This can also happen from a change in the political regime.Everyone would like to be a dictator if only he could.The winners of capitalism want to continue the system the losers think about abandoning the system.

The overturning of the balance of power.The entertainment industry takes over political influence.This is the new civilization I am building.Every action is considered by others as a signal.Be careful what signals you send to the world.

Maybe he is just crazy and what he understands is just randomness.Our society is based on the rule of reciprocation.

Can we trust the obstacle they put in front of our goals?

The human animal is good with violence in order to survive.

Game theory allways helped our understanding of the depths of human nature.

Alice was beginning to get very tired of sitting by her sister on the bank, and of having nothing to do: once or twice she had peeped into the book her sister was reading, but it had no pictures or conversations in it, 'and what is the use of a book,' thought Alice 'without pictures orconversation?'
So she was considering in her own mind (as well as she could, for the hot day made her feel very sleepy and stupid), whether the pleasure of making a daisy-chain would be worth the trouble of getting up and

picking the daisies, when suddenly a
White Rabbit with pink eyes ran
close by her.
There was nothing so VERY
remarkable in that; nor did Alice
think it so
VERY much out of the way to hear
the Rabbit say to itself, 'Oh dear!
Oh dear! I shall be late!' (when she
thought it over afterwards, it
occurred to her that she ought to
have wondered at this, but at the
time
it all seemed quite natural); but when
the Rabbit actually TOOK A
WATCH
OUT OF ITS WAISTCOAT-
POCKET, and looked at it, and then
hurried on,
Alice started to her feet, for it
flashed across her mind that she had
never before seen a rabbit with either
a waistcoat-pocket, or a watch

to take out of it, and burning with
curiosity, she ran across the field
after it, and fortunately was just in
time to see it pop down a large
rabbit-hole under the hedge.
In another moment down went Alice
after it, never once considering how
in the world she was to get out again.
The rabbit-hole went straight on like
a tunnel for some way, and then
dipped suddenly down, so suddenly
that Alice had not a moment to think
about stopping herself before she
found herself falling down a very
deep
well.
Either the well was very deep, or she
fell very slowly, for she had
plenty of time as she went down to
look about her and to wonder what
was
going to happen next. First, she tried
to look down and make out what

she was coming to, but it was too
dark to see anything; then she
looked at the sides of the well, and
noticed that they were filled with
cupboards and book-shelves; here
and there she saw maps and pictures
hung upon pegs. She took down a jar
from one of the shelves as
she passed; it was labelled
'ORANGE MARMALADE', but to
her great
disappointment it was empty: she did
not like to drop the jar for fear
of killing somebody, so managed to
put it into one of the cupboards as
she fell past it.
'Well!' thought Alice to herself, 'after
such a fall as this, I shall
think nothing of tumbling down
stairs! How brave they'll all think me
at
home! Why, I wouldn't say anything
about it, even if I fell off the top

of the house!' (Which was very likely true.) Down, down, down. Would the fall NEVER come to an end! 'I wonder how many miles I've fallen by this time?' she said aloud. 'I must be getting somewhere near the centre of the earth. Let me see: that would be four thousand miles down, I think--' (for, you see, Alice had learnt several things of this sort in her lessons in the schoolroom, and though this was not a VERY good opportunity for showing off her knowledge, as there was no one to listen to her, still it was good practice to say it over) '--yes, that's about the right distance--but then I wonder what Latitude or Longitude I've got to?' (Alice had no idea what Latitude was, or Longitude either, but thought they were nice grand words to say.)

Presently she began again. 'I wonder
if I shall fall right THROUGH the
earth! How funny it'll seem to come
out among the people that walk with
their heads downward! The
Antipathies, I think--' (she was rather
glad
there WAS no one listening, this
time, as it didn't sound at all the
right word) '--but I shall have to ask
them what the name of the country
is, you know. Please, Ma'am, is this
New Zealand or Australia?' (and
she tried to curtsey as she spoke--
fancy CURTSEYING as you're
falling
through the air! Do you think you
could manage it?) 'And what an
ignorant little girl she'll think me for
asking! No, it'll never do to
ask: perhaps I shall see it written up
somewhere.'

Down, down, down. There was
nothing else to do, so Alice soon
began
talking again. 'Dinah'll miss me very
much to-night, I should think!'
(Dinah was the cat.) 'I hope they'll
remember her saucer of milk at
tea-time. Dinah my dear! I wish you
were down here with me! There are
no
mice in the air, I'm afraid, but you
might catch a bat, and that's very
like a mouse, you know. But do cats
eat bats, I wonder?' And here Alice
began to get rather sleepy, and went
on saying to herself, in a dreamy
sort of way, 'Do cats eat bats? Do
cats eat bats?' and sometimes, 'Do
bats eat cats?' for, you see, as she
couldn't answer either question,
it didn't much matter which way she
put it. She felt that she was dozing
off, and had just begun to dream that
she was walking hand in hand with

Dinah, and saying to her very
earnestly, 'Now, Dinah, tell me the
truth:
did you ever eat a bat?' when
suddenly, thump! thump! down she
came upon
a heap of sticks and dry leaves, and
the fall was over.
Alice was not a bit hurt, and she
jumped up on to her feet in a
moment:
she looked up, but it was all dark
overhead; before her was another
long passage, and the White Rabbit
was still in sight, hurrying down it.
There was not a moment to be lost:
away went Alice like the wind, and
was just in time to hear it say, as it
turned a corner, 'Oh my ears
and whiskers, how late it's getting!'
She was close behind it when she
turned the corner, but the Rabbit was
no longer to be seen: she found

herself in a long, low hall, which was lit up by a row of lamps hanginfrom the roof.

There were doors all round the hall, but they were all locked; and when Alice had been all the way down one side and up the other, trying every door, she walked sadly down the middle, wondering how she was ever to

get out again.

Suddenly she came upon a little three-legged table, all made of solid glass; there was nothing on it except a tiny golden key, and Alice's first thought was that it might belong to one of the doors of the hall; but, alas! either the locks were too large, or the key was too small, but at any rate it would not open any of them. However, on the second time round, she came upon a low curtain she had not noticed before, and

behind it was a little door about
fifteen inches high: she tried the
little golden key in the lock, and to
her great delight it fitted!
Alice opened the door and found that
it led into a small passage, not
much larger than a rat-hole: she knelt
down and looked along the passage
into the loveliest garden you ever
saw. How she longed to get out of
that dark hall, and wander about
among those beds of bright flowers
and
those cool fountains, but she could
not even get her head through the
doorway; 'and even if my head
would go through,' thought poor
Alice, 'it
would be of very little use without
my shoulders. Oh, how I wish I
could
shut up like a telescope! I think I
could, if I only know how to begin.'

For, you see, so many out-of-the-
way things had happened lately,
that Alice had begun to think that
very few things indeed were really
impossible.
There seemed to be no use in waiting
by the little door, so she went
back to the table, half hoping she
might find another key on it, or at
any rate a book of rules for shutting
people up like telescopes: this
time she found a little bottle on it,
('which certainly was not here
before,' said Alice,) and round the
neck of the bottle was a paper
label, with the words 'DRINK ME'
beautifully printed on it in large
letters.
It was all very well to say 'Drink me,'
but the wise little Alice was
not going to do THAT in a hurry.
'No, I'll look first,' she said, 'and
see whether it's marked "poison" or
not'; for she had read several nice

little histories about children who had got burnt, and eaten up by wild beasts and other unpleasant things, all because they WOULD not remember

the simple rules their friends had taught them: such as, that a red-hot poker will burn you if you hold it too long; and that if you cut your finger VERY deeply with a knife, it usually bleeds; and she had never forgotten that, if you drink much from a bottle marked 'poison,' it i'What a curious feeling!' said Alice; 'I must be shutting up like a telescope.'

And so it was indeed: she was now only ten inches high, and her face brightened up at the thought that she was now the right size for going through the little door into that lovely garden. First, however, she waited for a few minutes to see if she was going to shrink any further:

she felt a little nervous about this;
'for it might end, you know,' said
Alice to herself, 'in my going out
altogether, like a candle. I wonder
what I should be like then?' And she
tried to fancy what the flame of a
candle is like after the candle is
blown out, for she could not
remember
ever having seen such a thing.
After a while, finding that nothing
more happened, she decided on
going
into the garden at once; but, alas for
poor Alice! when she got to the
door, she found she had forgotten the
little golden key, and when she
went back to the table for it, she
found she could not possibly reach
it: she could see it quite plainly
through the glass, and she tried her
best to climb up one of the legs of
the table, but it was too slippery;

and when she had tired herself out
with trying, the poor little thing
sat down and cried.
'Come, there's no use in crying like
that!' said Alice to herself,
rather sharply; 'I advise you to leave
off this minute!' She generally
gave herself very good advice,
(though she very seldom followed
it),
and sometimes she scolded herself so
severely as to bring tears into
her eyes; and once she remembered
trying to box her own ears for having
cheated herself in a game of croquet
she was playing against herself,
for this curious child was very fond
of pretending to be two people.
'But it's no use now,' thought poor
Alice, 'to pretend to be two people!
'Would it be of any use, now,'
thought Alice, 'to speak to this
mouse?

Everything is so out-of-the-way
down here, that I should think very
likely it can talk: at any rate, there's
no harm in trying.' So she
began: 'O Mouse, do you know the
way out of this pool? I am very tired
of swimming about here, O Mouse!'
(Alice thought this must be the right
way of speaking to a mouse: she had
never done such a thing before, but
she remembered having seen in her
brother's Latin Grammar, 'A mouse--
of
a mouse--to a mouse--a mouse--O
mouse!') The Mouse looked at her
rather
inquisitively, and seemed to her to
wink with one of its little eyes,
but it said nothing.
'Perhaps it doesn't understand
English,' thought Alice; 'I daresay it's
a French mouse, come over with
William the Conqueror.' (For, with
all

her knowledge of history, Alice had no very clear notion how long ago anything had happened.) So she began again: 'Ou est ma chatte?' which
was the first sentence in her French lesson-book. The Mouse gave a sudden leap out of the water, and seemed to quiver all over with fright. 'Oh, I beg your pardon!' cried Alice hastily, afraid that she had hurt the poor animal's feelings. 'I quite forgot you didn't like cats."But who is to give the prizes?' quite a chorus of voices asked.
'Why, SHE, of course,' said the Dodo, pointing to Alice with one finger;
and the whole party at once crowded round her, calling out in a confused way, 'Prizes! Prizes!'
Alice had no idea what to do, and in despair she put her hand in her

pocket, and pulled out a box of comfits, (luckily the salt water had not got into it), and handed them round as prizes. There was exactly one

a-piece all round.

'But she must have a prize herself, you know,' said the Mouse.

'Of course,' the Dodo replied very gravely. 'What else have you got in your pocket?' he went on, turning to Alice.

'Only a thimble,' said Alice sadly.

'Hand it over here,' said the Dodo.

Then they all crowded round her once more, while the Dodo solemnly presented the thimble, saying 'We beg your acceptance of this elegant thimble'; and, when it had finished this short speech, they all cheered.

Alice thought the whole thing very absurd, but they all looked so grave that she did not dare to laugh; and, as she could not think of anything to say, she simply bowed, and took the thimble, looking as solemn as she could.

The next thing was to eat the comfits: this caused some noise and confusion, as the large birds complained that they could not taste theirs, and the small ones choked and had to be patted on the back.

However, it was over at last, and they sat down again in a ring, and begged the Mouse to tell them something more.

'You promised to tell me your history, you know,' said Alice, 'and why it is you hate--C and D,' she added in a whisper, half afraid that it would be offended again.

'Mine is a long and a sad tale!' said the Mouse, turning to Alice, and sighing. 'Not QUITE right, I'm afraid,' said Alice, timidly; 'some of the words have got altered.'

'It is wrong from beginning to end,'
said the Caterpillar decidedly, and
there was silence for some minutes.
The Caterpillar was the first to
speak.

'What size do you want to be?' it
asked.

'Oh, I'm not particular as to size,'
Alice hastily replied; 'only one
doesn't like changing so often, you
know.'

'I DON'T know,' said the Caterpillar.

Alice said nothing: she had never
been so much contradicted in her life
before, and she felt that she was
losing her temper.

'Are you content now?' said the
Caterpillar.

'Well, I should like to be a LITTLE
larger, sir, if you wouldn't mind,'
said Alice: 'three inches is such a
wretched height to be.'

'It is a very good height indeed!' said
the Caterpillar angrily, rearing
itself upright as it spoke (it was
exactly three inches high).
'But I'm not used to it!' pleaded poor
Alice in a piteous tone. And
she thought of herself, 'I wish the
creatures wouldn't be so easily
offended!'
'You'll get used to it in time,' said the
Caterpillar; and it put the
hookah into its mouth and began
smoking again.
This time Alice waited patiently until
it chose to speak again. In
a minute or two the Caterpillar took
the hookah out of its mouth
and yawned once or twice, and
shook itself. Then it got down off the
mushroom, and crawled away in the
grass, merely remarking as it went,
'One side will make you grow taller,
and the other side will make you
grow shorter.'

'One side of WHAT? The other side of WHAT?' thought Alice to herself. 'Of the mushroom,' said the Caterpillar, just as if she had asked it aloud; and in another moment it was out of sight. Let $\Gamma = (K, S, v)$ be a game to n–players, with K the set of players $k = 1, ..., n$. The finite set Sk of

cardinality $lk \in N$ is the set of pure strategies of each player where $k \in K$, $skjk \in Sk$, $jk = 1, ..., lk$ and $S = \Pi KSk$ represents the set of pure strategy profiles with $s \in S$ an element of that set, $l = l1, l2, ..., ln$ represents the cardinality of S,[12, 43, 55, 56]. The vector function $v : S \rightarrow Rn$ associates every profile $s \in S$, where the vector of utilities $v(s) = (v1(s), ..., vn(s))T$, and $vk(s)$ designates the utility of the player k facing the profile s. In order to understand calculus easier, we write the function vk(s) in one explicit way vk(s) = vk(j1, j2, ..., jn).The matrix vn,l represents all points of the Cartesian product $\Pi_{k\in K}S_k$. The vector vk(s) is the k− column of v. If the mixed strategies are allowed then we have:

$\Delta(S_k) =$

(

$p_k \in R^{l_k}$:

X_{l_k}

$j_k=1$

p_k

$j_k = 1$

)

the unit simplex of the mixed strategies of player $k \in K$, and $p_k =$ (pk

jk) the probability vector. The set of profiles in mixed strategies is the polyhedron Δ with $\Delta = \Pi_{k\in K}$ $\Delta(S_k)$, where p = (p1j

1, p2j

2 ..., pnj

n), and

pk = (pk1

, pk2

, ..., pk

ln)T . Using the Kronecker product

$\otimes$ it is possible to write1:

$p = p1 \otimes p2 \otimes .. \otimes pk-1 \otimes pk \otimes pk+1 \otimes$

$... \otimes pn$

$p(-k) = p1 \otimes p2 \otimes .. \otimes$

$pk-1 \otimes lk \otimes pk+1 \otimes ... \otimes pn$

lk = (1, 1, ..., 1)T ,

£

lk¤

lk,1

ok = (0, 0, ..., 0)T ,

£

ok¤

lk,1

where

lk = (1, 1, ..., 1)T ,

£

lk¤

lk,1

$ok = (0, 0, ..., 0)T$,

£

ok¤

lk,1

The n– dimensional function u : $\Delta \to$ Rn associates with every profile in mixed strategies the vector of expected utilities

$u(p) =$

3

u1 (p, v(s)) , ..., un (p, v(s))

'T

where uk(p, v(s)) is the expected utility of the player k. Every ukj

k

= ukj

k

(p(−k), v(s)) represents the expected utility for each player's strategy and the vector uk is noted uk

= (uk1

, uk2

, ..., uk

n)T .

uk =

Xlk

jk=1

ukj

k

(p(−k), v(s))pk

jk

u = v0p

uk =

i

lk ⊗vk¢

p(−k)

The triplet (K,Δ, u(p)) designates the extension of the game Γ with the mixed strategies. We get Nash's equilibrium (the maximization of utility [3, 43, 55, 56, 57]) if and only if, ∀k, p, the inequality uk(p∗) ≥ uk(

i

pk

¢

∗ , p(−k)) is respected. **Theorem 1** *(Minimum Entropy Theorem). The*

game entropy is minimum only in mixed strategy Nash's equilibrium. The entropy minimization program Minp (
P

k Hk(p)), *is equal to the standard deviation minimization program* Minp
(Πkσk(p)), *when*
3

ukj
k
ʹ

has gaussian density function or multinomial logit.

According to Hayek, equilibrium refers to the order state or minimum entropy. The order state is the opposite of entropy (disorder measure). There are some intellectual influences and historical events which inspired Hayek to develop the idea of a spontaneous order. Here we present the technical tools needed in order to study the order state.

Case 1 *If the probability density of a variable X is normal:* $N(\mu k, \sigma k)$, *then its entropy is minimum for the minimum standard deviation* $(Hk)\min \Leftrightarrow (\sigma k)\min. \; \forall\, k = 1, ..., n.$

Proof. Let the entropy function $Hk =$ –

$R +\infty$

$-\infty$

$p(x) \ln(p(x))dx$ and $p(x)$ the normal density function.

Writing this entropy function in terms of minimum standard deviation we have.

$Hk = -$

$Z +\infty$

$-\infty$

$p(x)$

$\square$

$\square \ln$

$$\tilde{A} \frac{1}{2\pi\sigma^2_k} \tilde{A} \frac{x - u_k}{\sqrt{2}\sigma_k} \Box \Box dx$$

Ã

1 p

2πσ2

k

!

−

Ã

x − uk

√2σk

!2

□

□dx

developing the integral we haveTable 1. Quantum Mechanic and Game Theory properties

Quantum Mechanics

Particle: $k = 1, ..., n$

Quantum element

Interaction

Quantum state: $j = 1, ..., l_k$

Energy e

Superposition of states

State function

Probabilistic and optimal nature

Uncertainty Principle
Matrix operators
Variational Calculus,
Information Theory
Complexity
variety: number of particles n
variability: number of interactions n!
quantitative: Mathematical model
Observable value: E [e]
The entities communicate efficiently
Entropy
Game Theory
Player : $k = 1, ..., n$
Player type
Interaction
Strategy: $j = 1, ..., lk$
Utility u
Superposition of strategies
Utility function
Probabilistic and optimal nature
Minimum Entropy
Matrix operators
Optimal Control,
Information Theory

Complexity

variety: number of players n

variability: number of interactions n!

quantitative: Mathematical model

Observable value: E [u]

The players interact efficiently

Minimum Entropy

Let $k = 1, ..., n$ be players with lk strategies for every one $jk = mk1, ..., mkl$

k. According to the theorem of *Minimum Dispersion,* the utility ukj k, converges to Nash's equilibria and follows a normal probability density

$$\rho k(u) = e^{-\frac{1}{2}\left(\frac{u}{\sigma k} - \frac{\mu k}{\sigma k}\right)^2} \sigma k \sqrt{2\pi}$$

, where the expected utility is E

h

ukj

k

i

$= \mu k$. **Axiom 1** *At a fixed time* to ,
*the state of a physical system is
defined by specifying a ket* |ψ(to)i
beloging to
the state space (Hilbert space) V.
Axiom 2 *Every measurable physical
quantity* Λ *is described by the
operator* A *acting in* V ; *this
operator*
is an observable parameter.
Axiom 3 *The only possible result of
the measurement of a physical
quantity* Λ *is one of the eigenvalues
of*
the corresponding observable A.
Axiom 4 *When a physical quantity* Λ
*is measured on a system in the
normalized state* |ψ(t)i =

P

cj

ϕj

,

the probability P(bj) *of obtaining the non-degenerate eigenvalue* cj *of the corresponding observable* A *is:*
P(cj) =

ϕj,
ψ
 ⎯ 2 *where*

ϕj

is the normalized eigen vector of A *associated with the eigen value* cj.
Let n be players with k = 1, ..., n , lk strategies and mkj
k ∈ Mk
jk of each player k. Remember some basic definitions about probability and stochastic calculus.
A probability space is a triple (Ω,=, P) consisting of [10, 13, 30]:

• A set Ω that represents the set of all possible outcomes of a certain random experiment.

• A family $=$ of subsets of Ω with a structure of σ-algebra:

– $\emptyset \in =$

– $A \in = \Rightarrow A_c \in =$

– $A_1, A_2, ... \in = \Rightarrow \cup_{i=1}^{\infty} A_i \in =$

• A function $P : \Omega \rightarrow [0, 1]$ such that: **Definition 3** *A stochastic process* $X = \{X(t), t \in T\}$ *is a collection of random variables on a common probability space* $(\Omega, =, P)$ *indexed by a parameter* $t \in T \subset R,$ *which we usually interpret as time [10, 27-30]. It can thus be formulated as a function* $X : T \times \Omega \rightarrow R.$ The relationship between Time Series and Game Theory appears when we apply the entropy minimization theorem (EMT). This theorem (EMT) is a way to analyze the Nash-

Hayek equilibrium in mixed strategies.

Introducing the elements rationality and equilibrium in the domain of time series can be a big help, because it allows us to study the human behavior reflected and registered in historical data. The main contributions of this complementary focus on time series has a relationship with Econophysics and rationality. Human behavior evolves and is the result of learning. The objective of learning is stability and optimal equilibrium. Due to the above-mentioned, we can affirm that if learning is optimal then the convergence to equilibrium is faster than when the learning is sub-optimal. Introducing elements of Nash's equilibrium

in time series will allow us to
evaluate learning and the
convergence to equilibrium through
the study of
historical data (time series).
One of the branches of Physics
called Quantum Mechanics was
pioneered using Heisemberg's
uncertainty
principle. This paper is simply the
application of this principle in Game
Theory and Time Series.
Econophysics is a newborn branch of
the scientific development that
attempts to establish the analogies
between Economics and Physics, see
Mantenga and Stanley [33]. The
establishment of analogies is a
creative way of applying the idea of
cooperative equilibrium. The product
of this cooperative equilibrium
will produce synergies between these
two sciences. From my point of
view, the power of physics is the

capacity of equilibrium formal treatment in stochastic dynamic systems. On the other hand, the power of

Economics is the formal study of rationality, cooperative and non-cooperative equilibrium.

Econophysics is the beginning of a unification stage of the systemic approach of scientific thought. I show

that it is the beginning of a unification stage but remains to create synergies with the rest of the sciences.

Let $\{x_t\}_{t=-\infty}^{t=\infty}$

be a covariance-stationary process with the mean $E[x_t] = \mu$ and jth covariance γ_j

$E[(x_t - \mu)(x_{t-j} - \mu)] = \gamma_j$ Britain was readying Sunday for the flood of secret US diplomatic cables about to be published by the WikiLeaks website, with politicians gearing up to hear what US officials really thought of them.

Prime Minister David Cameron's governing Conservative-Liberal coalition and members of the former Labour administrations of his precessors Gordon Brown and Tony Blair were bracing for the flood of millions of documents.

Some Sunday newspapers quoted government sources as saying that whatever might be coming about Cameron and his coalition, it was nothing compared to what US officials thought of his predecessor Brown.

Several reports said that US ambassador Louis Susman had briefed British officials about the likely contents of the files, amid fears the cables will embarrass both the United States and its allies.

The documents could include reports from officials in Washington and diplomatic posts around the world about issues on which Britain and the United States have collaborated closely, including the wars in Iraq and Afghanistan.

The Sunday Times newspaper quoted one government official as warning that British citizens in Muslim countries could be targeted in a violent backlash over any perceived "anti-Islamic" views expressed.

"The concern of the UK government is that some of the diplomatic conversations may contain certain phrases (critical) of certain sensitive places by either the US or us in which Britain might be portrayed as

being hand in glove with the Great
Satan to attack Islam," the official
was quoted as saying.

"There is a nervousness that that
might inflame the hotheads".

The Ministry of Defence has urged
newspaper editors to "bear in mind"
the national security implications of
publishing any of the files.

British officials said some
information might be subject to
voluntary agreements between the
government and the media to
withhold sensitive data governing
military operations and the
intelligence services.

Britain's biggest-selling newspaper
the News of the World said
WikiLeaks' Australian founder had a
heavy responsibility on his

shoulders.

"Computer nerd Julian Assange is on the run this weekend as he prepares to post stolen state secrets on the Internet," the tabloid said in its editorial.

"Things have got a little to hot for the self-styled 'James Bond of journalism'.

"But there may be no hiding place for the hundreds of brave souls his WikiLeaks website threatens to expose."

The Mail on Sunday editorial said there was a "grim irony" in the latest WikiLeaks disclosures.

"Modern states have been great enthusiasts for recording the details of their subjects on databases, brusquely ignoring fears that such things endanger privacy," the tabloid said.

"But had these matters been kept out of vulnerable databases, the problem almost certainly would not have arisen, at least on this scale."

The Sunday Express newspaper said governments needed to get to grips with the fact that it was now harder to keep communications secret in the Internet age. Recall that the partition function for the canonical ensemble at temperature $\beta-1$ is given by $Z = R$ $\exp(-\beta E)d\omega(E)$, where $\omega(E)$ is a "density of states" measure, which does not depend on β. Then one computes the average energy $< E >= -\partial$ $\partial\beta \log Z$, the entropy $S = \beta < E > + \log Z$, and the fluctuation $\sigma = \langle (E - \langle E \rangle)^2 \rangle = \frac{\partial^2}{(\partial \beta)^2} \log Z$.

Now fix a closed manifold M with a probability measure m, and suppose that our system is described by a metric $g_{ij}(\tau)$, which depends on the temperature τ according to equation $(g_{ij})_\tau = 2(R_{ij} + \nabla_i \nabla_j f)$, where $dm = u\,dV$, $u = (4\pi\tau)^{-\frac{n}{2}} e^{-f}$, and the partition function is given by $\log Z = \int_M \left(-f + \frac{n}{2}\right) dm$.

(We do not discuss here what assumptions on g_{ij} guarantee that the corresponding "density of states" measure can be found) Then we compute

$$\langle E \rangle = -\tau^2 \int_M \left(R + |\nabla f|^2 - \frac{n}{2\tau}\right)$$

)dm,

$$S = -Z_M$$

$$(\tau (R + |\nabla f|^2) + f - n)dm,$$

$$\sigma = 2\tau 4 Z_M |R_{ij} + \nabla_i\nabla_j f -$$

$$\frac{1}{2\tau}$$

$$g_{ij}|^2 dm$$

Alternatively, we could prescribe the evolution equations by replacing the t-derivatives by minus τ-derivatives in (3.3), and get the same formulas for

$Z, < E >, S, \sigma$, with dm replaced by udV.

Clearly, σ is nonnegative; it vanishes only on a gradient shrinking soliton. $< E >$ is nonnegative as well, whenever the flow exists for all sufficiently

small $\tau > 0$ (by proposition 1.2). Furthermore, if (a) u tends to a δ-function

as $\tau \to 0$, or (b) u is a limit of a sequence of functions u_i, such that

eachThe computation suggests that this integral, which we will call the reduced

volume and denote by $\tilde{V}(\tau(q))$, should be increasing as τ decreases. A rigorous

proof of this monotonicity is given in the next section.

6.4* The first geometric interpretation of Hamilton's Harnack expressions

was found by Chow and Chu [C-Chu 1,2]; they construct a potentially degenerate riemannian metric on M×R, which potentially satisfies the Ricci

soliton equation; our construction is, in a certain sense, dual to theirs.

Our formula for the reduced volume resembles the expression in Huisken monotonicity formula for the mean curvature flow [Hu]; however, in our case the monotonicity is in the opposite direction.

The New Strategic Doctrines of NATO

NATO 2020: Assured Security; Dynamic Engagement

Analysis and Recommendations of the Group of Experts on a New Strategic Concept for NATO

Introduction

At their Summit in Strasbourg/Kehl in April, 2009, Alliance leaders directed Secretary General Anders Fogh Rasmussen to convene a broadly-based group of qualified experts to prepare the ground for a new NATO Strategic Concept. The Group of Experts, led by its chair Madeleine K. Albright (United States) and vice-chair Jeroen van der Veer (The Netherlands), began work in September 2009. In line with its mandate to encourage an open discussion of NATO's organisation and purpose, the Group engaged in an extensive series of seminars and consultations with scholars and officials, civilian and military alike, from within and outside the Alliance. The Group, which submitted an interim statement to NATO's governing body (the North Atlantic Council) on November 24, 2009, presents now its final report. The document includes a summary of findings (Part One) and a more detailed discussion of leading issues (Part Two). The analysis and recommendations are intended to assist the Secretary General in drafting a new Strategic Concept for submission to NATO heads of government at the November 2010 summit in Lisbon.

The Group of Experts is grateful to the hundreds of men and women who assisted in its work, including

Secretary General Rasmussen and his planning staff (headed by Dr. Jamie Shea), the governments of the Alliance and its partners, seminar hosts and participants, military and civilian advisers, and all who contributed their ideas and thoughts.

Part One: Summary of Findings

New Perils, New Resolve

The North Atlantic Treaty Organisation (NATO) enters the second decade of the twenty-first century as an essential source of stability in an uncertain and unpredictable world. Looking ahead, the Alliance has ample grounds for confidence. The democratic principles that initially brought it together remain valid. The Cold War rivalry that once stirred fears of nuclear Armageddon has long since disappeared. NATO's role in maintaining the unity, security and freedom of the Euro-Atlantic region is ongoing. Its status as the globe's most successful political-military Alliance is unchallenged. Yet NATO's past accomplishments provide no guarantee for the future. Between now and 2020, it will be tested by the emergence of new dangers, the many-sided demands of complex operations, and the challenge of organising itself efficiently in an era where rapid responses are vital, versatility critical, and resources tight.

NATO needs a new Strategic Concept because the world has changed significantly since 1999, when the current concept was adopted. Most dramatically, the 9/11 and subsequent attacks demonstrated the deadly connection between technology and terror, triggering a response that has drawn NATO troops far from home, illuminated the need for timely intelligence-sharing, and complicated planning for defence. Further, the global nuclear non-proliferation regime is under increasing stress; incidents of instability along Europe's periphery have revived historic tensions; innovative modes of gathering, sending and storing information have brought with them new vulnerabilities; the security implications of piracy, energy supply risks and environmental neglect have become more evident; and a worldwide economic crisis has spawned widespread budgetary concerns. Meanwhile, the Alliance has grown to twenty-eight, enlarging both NATO's capabilities and its commitments. Clearly, the time is right to take a fresh look at the

Alliance's missions, procedures and plans.

The development of a new Strategic Concept provides an opportunity to introduce NATO to populations who know little about it and who may be sceptical about the organisation's relevance to their lives. Although NATO is busier than it has ever been, its value is less obvious to many than in the past. Alliance leaders must use this opening to highlight NATO's many contributions to international stability and peace. Otherwise, the organisation could fail to retain the public backing and financial support it must have to perform critical tasks well.

The new Strategic Concept must also serve as an invocation of political will or -- to put it another way -- a renewal of vows, on the part of each member. Threats to the interests of the Alliance come from the outside, but the organisation's vigour could as easily be sapped from within. The increasing complexity of the global political environment has the potential to gnaw away at Alliance cohesion; economic headaches can distract attention from security needs; old rivalries could resurface; and the possibility is real of a damaging imbalance between the military contributions of some members and that of others. NATO states cannot allow twenty-first century dangers to do what past perils could not: divide their leaders and weaken their collective resolve. Thus, the new Strategic Concept must clarify both what NATO should be doing for each Ally and what each Ally should be doing for NATO.

NATO's Legacy of Success

The Alliance began work in 1949 when the Cold War was just underway, sharply dividing the democratic West from a communist East. NATO's purpose, set out in the North Atlantic Treaty, was to protect the freedom and safety of its members. In Article 4, Allies pledged "to consult together whenever, in the opinion of any of them, the territorial integrity, political independence or security of any of the Parties is threatened." In Article 5, members agreed "that an armed attack against one or more of them in Europe or North America shall be considered an attack against them all."

Until 1989, when the Berlin Wall fell, NATO ensured the unity of the West by defending against possible attack from the communist bloc and by supporting democratic principles against totalitarian ideologies. NATO's resolve helped to keep the continent at peace and ultimately to facilitate the reunification of Germany and a new beginning for millions of people in Central and Eastern Europe.

In the 1990s, NATO's primary goal (in association with the European Union (EU)) was to consolidate a Europe whole and free. For the first time, it engaged in military action, putting a halt to ethnic cleansing in the Balkans. The Cold War's end enabled the Alliance to establish partnerships with former adversaries, including Russia, and to admit new members who embraced democratic values and who could contribute to NATO's collective security. The result was a Europe more democratic, united, and peaceful than it had ever been.

The turn of the century brought with it new and varied challenges for the Alliance. In earlier decades, NATO's defence preparations emphasised the massing of troops to deter or repel a cross-border attack. Today, Alliance members remain concerned about the possibility that regional disputes or efforts at political intimidation could undermine security along its borders. However, NATO must also cope with hazards of a more volatile and less predictable nature -- including acts of terrorism, the proliferation of nuclear and other advanced weapons technologies, cyber attacks directed against modern communications systems, the sabotage of energy pipelines, and the disruption of critical maritime supply routes. Often, an effective defence against these unconventional security threats must begin well beyond the territory of the Alliance.

Already, NATO has responded to this new reality by assisting the government of Afghanistan in its fight against violent extremism, combating piracy in the Gulf of Aden, contributing to seaborne security in the Mediterranean, training and equipping Iraqi defence forces, and helping to construct more stable societies in Bosnia-Herzegovina and Kosovo. As this list indicates, shifting defence imperatives bring with them new needs -- for a transformation in military capabilities, a more sophisticated approach to NATO partnerships, more extensive security consultations, and a more streamlined and efficient Alliance structure.

A new Strategic Concept must recognise the urgency of further change while remaining true to the founding ideals that bind the Alliance together and that have earned for it a positive international reputation. This calls for a blend of reaffirmation and renovation aimed at creating the optimum mix of old and new.

An Enduring Foundation

In 1967, a team comparable to today's Group of Experts was assembled under the leadership of Belgian Foreign Minister Pierre Harmel. The Harmel report observed that "The North Atlantic Treaty area cannot be treated in isolation from the rest of the world." It also described NATO as an Alliance that is "constantly adapting itself to changing conditions" and that had two core functions: the first to maintain the strength and solidarity required to deter aggression and the second to pursue a more stable long term political environment. Forty-three years later, this description still fits. NATO is an ever-evolving part of an also-evolving international security framework; its mission of self defence has always hinged, in part, on events beyond its borders. The fact that NATO troops are now deployed in distant locations is not a departure from NATO's fundamental purpose.

The Strategic Concept adopted in 1999 conformed to the security needs that had arisen during the first decade of the post-Cold War era. The document set forth a host of ideas that ring as true today and that should be reaffirmed in the 2010 Concept. These core building blocks include, but are not limited to, the following:

- NATO's central purpose is to safeguard -- by political and military means -- the freedom and security of all its members.
- The Alliance embodies the transatlantic link by which the security of North America is permanently tied to the security of Europe.
- the security of all Allies is indivisible: an attack on one is an attack on all.
- The combined military forces of the Alliance must be able to 1) deter any potential aggression against it and 2) ensure the political independence and territorial integrity of its members.
- Alliance success depends on the equitable sharing among

members of roles, risks and responsibilities, as well as benefits.

- NATO will make full use of its links to other countries and organisations to help prevent and mitigate crises.
- The stability, transparency, predictability, lower levels of armaments, and verification which can be provided by arms control and non-proliferation agreements support NATO's political and military efforts to achieve its strategic objectives.
- In fulfilling its purpose and fundamental security tasks, the Alliance will continue to respect the legitimate security interests of others, and seek the peaceful resolution of disputes as set out in the Charter of the United Nations.

As these assertions signify, the Alliance needs a new Strategic Concept, but it does not require wholesale change. NATO's fundamental identity, as the organisation that lends muscle and spine to democratic ideals, is constant. However, the NATO of 2020 will not be the same as the NATO of 1950, 1990, or even 2010. As the Alliance matures, it must prepare itself to confront an array of fresh perils.

Moving Toward NATO 2020

Reaffirming NATO's Core Commitment: Collective Defence. NATO's core commitment -- embodied in Article 5 of the North Atlantic Treaty -- is unchanged, but the requirements for fulfilling that commitment have shifted in shape. To remain credible, this pledge to shield member states from armed aggression must be backed up not only by basic military capabilities but also by the contingency planning, focused exercises, force readiness, and sound logistics required to preserve the confidence of Allies while minimizing the likelihood of miscalculation on the part of potential adversaries.

Protecting Against Unconventional Threats. Provided NATO stays vigilant, the prospect of direct military attack across the borders of the Alliance is slight, at least for the foreseeable future. We have learned, however, that in our era less conventional threats to the Alliance could arise from afar and still affect security at home. These dangers include attacks involving weapons of mass destruction, terrorist strikes, and efforts to harm society through cyber assaults or the unlawful disruption of critical supply lines. To guard against these threats, which may or may not reach the level of an Article 5 attack, NATO must update its approach to the defence of Alliance territory while also enhancing its ability to prevail in military operations and broader security missions beyond its borders.

Establishing Guidelines for Operations Outside Alliance Borders. For all its assets, NATO is by no means the sole answer to every problem affecting international security. NATO is a regional, not a global organisation; its authority and resources are limited and it has no desire to take on missions that other institutions and countries can handle successfully. Accordingly, the new Strategic Concept should prescribe guidelines for NATO as it makes decisions about when and where to apply its resources outside Alliance borders.

Creating the Conditions for Success in Afghanistan. NATO's mission in Afghanistan is the largest ever attempted by the Alliance. Every Ally is contributing to this operation and many have recently increased their participation. NATO countries are also donating generously to the economic and political development of the country. The Alliance is committed to the creation of an Afghanistan that is stable and that does not serve as a platform for international terrorist activity; it should continue working with its partners to achieve this strategically important objective. Looking to the future, the Allied experience in Afghanistan is a rich source of lessons to be learned.

Many of the principles that should be
featured in the new Strategic
Concept are in evidence. These
include the requirement for Alliance
cohesion, the desirability of unified
command, the value of effective
planning and public diplomacy, the
aptness of a comprehensive
civilian/military approach, and the
need to deploy forces at a strategic
distance for an extended period of
time.

**Consultations to Prevent or
Manage Crises.** Given the changing
character and growing variety of
dangers to the security of member
states, the Allies should make more
creative and regular use of the
consultations authorized by Article
4. These consultations, which
highlight the Alliance's function as a
political community, can be
important both for preventing and

managing crises and need not await an imminent Article 5 threat. Indeed, consultations are singularly well-suited to the review of unconventional dangers and to situations that might require an emergency international response. Article 4 provides an opportunity to share information, promote a convergence of views, avoid unpleasant surprises, and clear a path for successful action -- whether that action is of a diplomatic, precautionary, remedial, or coercive nature.

A New Era of Partnerships. The new Strategic Concept must recognize that, as NATO moves toward 2020, it will generally not operate alone. Partnerships, in all their diversity, will occupy a central place in the daily work of the Alliance. To make the most of this reality, NATO must strive to clarify and deepen relations with key partners, to establish new relationships where appropriate, to expand the range of partnership activities, and to understand that each partner and partnership must be dealt with on its own terms.

Participating in a Comprehensive Approach to Complex Problems. Healthy partnerships provide an opening for NATO to pursue solutions to complex problems that affect its security; in most instances, the preferred method will be a comprehensive approach that combines military and civilian elements. NATO is strong and versatile but it is by no means well-suited to every task. Other organisations, national governments and nongovernmental entities can lead the way toward such vital goals as economic reconstruction, political reconciliation, improved governance, and the strengthening of civil society. Depending on the needs in any particular case, NATO may serve as the principal organiser of a collaborative effort, or as a source of specialized assistance, or in some other complementary role.

Engaging with Russia. The NATO-Russia partnership was conceived as a means for fostering security in the Euro-Atlantic region; the Alliance remains dedicated to that goal. The principal forum for communication through the Alliance has been the NATO-Russia Council (NRC). This venue -- which has not always been adequately employed -- was designed to provide the means for preventing crises, analyzing events, broaching ideas, and agreeing on joint actions to deal with mutual concerns. Although the Alliance neither poses a military threat to Russia, nor considers Russia a military threat to the Alliance, doubts persist on both sides about the intentions and policies of the other.

Consistent with the NATO-Russia Founding Act, the new Strategic Concept should reaffirm NATO's desire to help build a cooperative Euro-Atlantic security order which includes security cooperation with Russia. Bearing this principle in mind, NATO should pursue a policy of engagement with Russia while reassuring all Allies that their security and interests will be defended. To this end, the Alliance should demonstrate its commitment to the NRC (and invite Russia to do the same) by focusing on opportunities for pragmatic collaboration in pursuit of such shared interests as nuclear non-proliferation, arms control, counter-terrorism, missile defence, effective crisis management, peace operations, maritime security, and the fight against trafficking in illegal drugs.

Maintaining the Open Door. Since the end of the Cold War, NATO's membership has expanded from sixteen members to twenty-eight. This open door policy has been an engine of progress towards a Europe whole and free and has contributed much to the collective security of Alliance members. Further enlargement has been under consideration in the western Balkans and with respect to Georgia and Ukraine. Consistent with Article 10 of the North Atlantic Treaty and the principles for enlargement, the process for states that have expressed their desire for membership should move forward as each state fulfils the requirements for membership. It should go without saying that NATO is an entirely voluntary organisation.

New Capabilities for a New Era (Military Transformation and Reform). NATO's military and political commitments will mean little unless matched by capabilities. The Strategic Concept should include a clear statement of defence priorities and be accompanied by an agreed set of essential new or improved capabilities and reforms. NATO forces must have the capacity to defend Alliance territory, undertake demanding missions at strategic distance, contribute to a more secure international environment, and respond to unpredictable contingencies when and where that is required. Thus, there is a continuing need to transform NATO forces from the powerful but static posture of the Cold War into a posture that is more flexible, mobile, and versatile. With resources stretched thin in almost every NATO capital, the Alliance must also make a firm commitment to smarter spending through a variety of efficiency and reform measures.

Nuclear Weapons Policy: Solidarity in Pursuit of Peace. As long as nuclear weapons exist, NATO should continue to maintain secure and reliable nuclear forces, with widely shared responsibility for deployment and operational support, at the minimum level required by the prevailing security environment. Any change in this policy, including in the geographic distribution of NATO nuclear deployments in Europe, should be made, as with other major decisions, by the Alliance as a whole.

The Strategic Concept should also affirm NATO's full support for efforts to prevent the proliferation of nuclear weapons, ensure that nuclear materials are handled in a safe and secure manner, and make progress towards a world free from the fear of nuclear war. In this spirit, the Alliance has dramatically curtailed the types and numbers of sub-strategic nuclear forces in Europe and should welcome consultations with Russia in pursuit of increased transparency and further mutual reductions.

The New Mission of Missile Defence. Defending against the threat of a possible ballistic missile attack from Iran has given birth to what has become, for NATO, an essential military mission. President

Obama's decision to deploy a phased adaptive missile defence will provide more effective, rapid and reliable coverage than earlier proposals. It also puts missile defence fully within a NATO context, with participation open to all Allies and all Allies to be protected. Missile defence is most effective when it is a joint enterprise and so cooperation throughout the Alliance and between NATO and its partners (especially Russia) is highly desirable.

Responding to the Rising Danger of Cyber Attacks. NATO must accelerate efforts to respond to the danger of cyber attacks by protecting its own communications and command systems, helping Allies to improve their ability to prevent and recover from attacks, and developing an array of cyber defence capabilities aimed at effective detection and deterrence.

Implementing Reforms to Create a More Agile Alliance. The Strategic Concept should authorize and encourage the Secretary General to move ahead with a farreaching agenda of administrative and other reforms aimed at producing an Alliance that is leaner, better able to make timely decisions, and more efficient and cost-effective.

Telling NATO's Story. As Allies prepare a new Strategic Concept, they should bear in mind how such a document will be read not only within the Euro-Atlantic community but in every region. NATO populations should be reminded that the Alliance serves their interests through the security it provides; people outside NATO should know that the organisation and its partners are working each day to build a safer world.

Vision and Purpose

Compared to its first decades, NATO between 2010 and 2020 is likely to appear less often on the centre stage of global affairs. Instead, it will be cast in a variety of roles, sometimes as a leader, at other times in a supporting capacity sharing the spotlight with partners and friends. All the while, it will need to keep a wary eye on dangers that could arise close to home, while maintaining a farsighted focus on how to respond to perils that might emerge at distant locations. For the Alliance of the 1960's, defence and détente were two sides of the same coin. For NATO 2020, the twin imperative is assured security for all its members and dynamic engagement beyond the treaty area to minimize threats.

To succeed, NATO must have the sustained commitment and united effort of its members. A seat at NATO's table is not an entitlement but an ongoing responsibility that each Ally must meet. Together, the Alliance must summon the resources needed to back its obligations with capabilities so that the full range of threats to its security are not only contained but also defeated or deterred.

Looking to the future, we know that global and regional risks must naturally command NATO's attention, but that these impermanent worries must never be allowed to define the organisation. In 1949, NATO members came together not because of the forces they feared, but because of their faith in each other and in the democratic values they embraced. In the years since, Allied leaders have learned that their Alliance must constantly adapt to the demands of political and technological change, but they have also learned what must not change. NATO's Strategic Concept must begin and end with NATO's founding ideals.

Part Two: Further Analysis and Recommendations

Chapter 1: The Security Environment

Background

Through its policies and actions, NATO has helped to forge for itself a zone of security, peace, and relative prosperity in a world that is more tumultuous and uncertain than when, in 1999, the previous Strategic

Concept was adopted. The Alliance remains a cornerstone of stability in the Euro-Atlantic region thanks to its political cohesion, commitment to mutual defence, and wide-ranging capabilities. Over the past two decades, it has successfully integrated twelve new members from Central and Eastern Europe, developed vital new partnerships, and taken on a number of missions that contribute daily to its own security and to that of the world.

It is difficult to offer detailed predictions about the next ten years. This should not be surprising. Even during the relatively rigid conditions of the Cold War, unforeseen events of major geopolitical import took place. In the current day, uncertainty is magnified by such factors as:

- The proliferation of nuclear and other weapons of mass destruction;
- The ambitions of international terrorist groups;
- The persistence of corrosive regional, national, ethnic, and religious rivalries;
- The world's increased reliance on potentially vulnerable information systems;
- The competition for petroleum and other strategic resources (thereby highlighting the importance of maritime security);
- Demographic changes that could aggravate such global problems as poverty, hunger, illegal immigration, and pandemic disease; and
- The accumulating consequences of environmental

degradation, including climate change.

Analysis

Despite the hectic pace and fluidity of modern life, sources of stability do exist. NATO, of course, is one such source but so is the vast network of economic and political connections that link the major world powers. Some of the global institutions that were established in previous decades may be showing signs of age, but they still provide the means for resolving international disputes in harmony with the rule of law. Although the spread of nuclear weapons is a growing worry, prominent international leaders profess their determination to confront it. Emerging global powers such as China, India and Brazil are asserting their rising influence in a peaceful manner. As NATO plans for the hazards of a new decade, it can do so with knowledge that its desire to live in concord with others is widely (if not universally) shared. There should be no question that our future is filled with dangers both known and unknown, but we should neither sell short nor take lightly the foundation for further progress that our predecessors have created.

Global Trends. Between now and 2020, the international security environment will change in ways both predictable and unforeseen. Certainly, the forces that come under the general heading of globalization can be counted upon to intensify. This will result in a rapid, if uneven, growth in cross-border flows of goods, services, people, technology, ideas, customs, crime, and weapons. This deepening interdependence will bring the world ever closer but not necessarily make populations more inclined to live in peace. Globalization has shown a tendency to empower some while marginalizing others, and has at times heightened the combustible tension between individual and group identity. Although it contributes to a steady rise in shared economic interests between and among countries, globalization provides no sure remedy for international suspicions and rivalry.

From a security standpoint, the most salient aspect of our era is that events in one part of the world are far more likely than in the past to have repercussions elsewhere. Anarchy in one country can create an opportunity for terrorists to find a safe haven from which to operate across any border. A nation that evades global norms and gets away with it creates a precedent that others might follow. A cyber attack that leads to chaos in one city may inspire copy-cat criminals in another. Due to the reach of modern media, even terrorist groups and pirate bands now have public relations specialists and NATO, when and wherever it acts (or fails to act), will do so with a global audience.

With the Cold War long since ended, NATO must find its place within a less centralized and more complicated international order. Its new role will be influenced by the emergence of specific threats from a diverse spectrum of possibilities. Such threats may be directed at the territory of Allies or at their citizens, economic lifelines, infrastructure, troops, and even their values. These dangers could come in the form of conventional attacks or provocative statements intended to serve as a means of political blackmail. They could arrive in forms with which we are familiar, or in hybrid variations that combine, for example, the stealth of a terrorist group with the power normally associated with a nation-state -- including purchased or purloined weapons of mass destruction.

Because of its visibility and power, NATO may well be called upon to respond to challenges that do not directly affect its security but that still matter to its citizens and that will contribute to the Alliance's international standing. These challenges could include the humanitarian consequences of a failed state, the devastation caused by a natural disaster, or the dangers posed by genocide or other massive violations of human rights.

Less predictable is the possibility that research breakthroughs will transform the technological battlefield. Allies and partners should be alert for potentially disruptive developments in such dynamic areas as information and communications technology, cognitive and biological sciences, robotics, and nanotechnology. The most destructive periods of history tend to be those when the means of aggression have gained the upper hand in the art of waging war.

Regional Trends. NATO and the EU remain the central pillars of stability and cooperation in the Euro-Atlantic region. This area of the world is hardly free of problems, but the likelihood of military conflict -- whether international or civil -- is relatively low. Lingering grievances do persist in the Caucasus and Balkans, however, and these will demand sustained international attention. Cooperation within the region will also be essential to deal with transnational aggravations that include trafficking in arms, drugs, and humans. Leaders are reminded, as well, of the potential for any part of the world to produce its share of home-grown terrorists.

Because of Russia's size and stature, it will inevitably play a prominent role in shaping the Euro-Atlantic security environment. On the positive side, Russia has shown an increased willingness to support the air and land transport of supplies to NATO forces in Afghanistan, has engaged in productive strategic arms control negotiations with the United States, and has expressed strong opposition to terrorism, piracy, and the further proliferation of nuclear weapons states. Experience teaches, however, that Russian and NATO leaders do not always view the same set of facts in the same way. Leaders in Moscow have expressed concerns about past and prospective NATO enlargement, while Allies have voiced concerns about possible attempts by Russia to engage in acts of political or economic intimidation. This combination of shared interests and strained feelings argues for a policy of active and constructive engagement both on NATO's part and Russia's.

The Strategic Concept can be instrumental in unifying the Allies' views on Russia, clarifying NATO's intentions towards Moscow, and laying the groundwork for more substantive cooperation. Because

Russia's future policies toward NATO remain difficult to predict, the Allies must pursue the goal of cooperation while also guarding against the possibility that Russia could decide to move in a more adversarial direction.

Several Central Asian governments have welcomed and supported NATO's engagement in Afghanistan as a contributor to regional stability. Obviously, the sustained insurgency in that country has implications far beyond its borders, beginning with neighbouring Pakistan -- which faces a serious and possibly growing terrorist threat of its own. The future direction of these two countries will do much to determine whether the danger posed by al-Qa'ida and its allies wanes over time. The evidence to date is that popular support for these terrorist organisations is low but that so, too, is public confidence in governments within the region. Thus, political reform and improved governance could be major contributors to a healthier security climate throughout Central Asia. If these changes do not materialize, the region will pose severe dangers both for those who live in it and for those who do not.

In the Middle East, three significant and interrelated trends will continue to affect Alliance security: 1) ongoing extremist violence; 2) simmering Arab-Israeli tensions; and 3) the policies of the government of Iran, including its unwillingness to comply with UN Security Council resolutions related to its nuclear programme. Iran's efforts to enrich nuclear fuel, develop nuclear weapons designs, and stockpile long-range ballistic missiles could create a major Article 5 threat to the Alliance in this decade. In addition, Iran's conventional weapons programmes, especially its anti-ship cruise missiles, raise concerns about the security of critical maritime trading routes. Given the abundant international diplomatic activity focused on Iran and the obscurity of Teheran's intentions, it is unclear whether the difficulties posed by Iran will multiply or diminish in the years ahead. NATO should do all it can to encourage the latter possibility, while preparing itself for the former.

In the Asia-Pacific, the major powers, which include Japan, the Republic of Korea, China, India, and Australia, all view regional stability as in their interests and are generally supportive of international norms. The two primary sources of instability are longstanding -- the rivalry between India and Pakistan, and the dangerous government of the People's Republic of North Korea (DPRK). The DPRK's nuclear weapons programme warrants particular attention.

Africa has made important economic gains in recent years accompanied by considerable progress in dealing with chronic plagues of civil strife, disease, and ineffective government. A number of serious trouble spots remain, however, including most prominently the Democratic Republic of the Congo, Somalia and Sudan. Although leaders in the region are determined to cope with their own problems through the African Union, Allies may receive requests for assistance with respect to peacekeeping missions, counter-terrorism activities, and military training.

The area of Latin America and the Caribbean, like North America, has its share of challenges with crime being among the more prominent. The Organization of American States is the principal regional body for both continents. Thus, with the possible exception of a humanitarian emergency, it is hard to foresee direct NATO involvement in this region.

Conclusions:

- Conventional military aggression against the Alliance or its members is unlikely but the possibility cannot be ignored.
- The most probable threats to Allies in the coming decade are unconventional. Three in particular stand out: 1) an attack by ballistic missile

(whether or not nuclear-armed); 2) strikes by international terrorist groups; and 3) cyber assaults of varying degrees of severity. A host of other threats also pose a risk, including disruptions to energy and maritime supply lines, the harmful consequences of global climate change, and financial crisis.

- The danger posed by unconventional threats has obvious implications for NATO preparedness, including its definition of security, its conception of what constitutes an Article 5 attack, its strategy for deterrence, its need for military transformation, its ability to make decisions rapidly, and its reliance for help on countries and organisations from outside the Alliance.

Chapter 2: Core Tasks

Background

NATO's overriding purpose, set out in the North Atlantic Treaty, is "to safeguard the freedom, common heritage, and civilisation" of its members. The treaty signatories proposed to achieve this objective by uniting "their efforts for collective defence and for the preservation of peace and security." These actions have always required that the Alliance perform certain core tasks the nature of which has evolved in keeping with alterations in the international security landscape. In the past two decades, as threats to the Euro-Atlantic region have grown more mobile and diverse, NATO has assumed new and broader missions that could hardly have been foreseen in 1949. However, these missions are fully consistent with the original objective of safeguarding the freedom of Alliance members.

Analysis and Recommendations

It is vital that Allies agree on what their core tasks are and on the need to maintain the capabilities required to fulfil them. NATO today is more active than at any previous time, yet its role in providing security is less obvious to many than it was during the Cold War. The new Strategic Concept offers an opportunity for reconciling differences of perspective and for dealing with novel situations. To this end, a fresh iteration of the core tasks of the Alliance is a necessary first step.

Recommendation:

1. The Group of Experts
   recommends that the 2010
   Strategic Concept should
   highlight the following quartet
   of core tasks:

First, the Alliance must maintain the ability to deter and defend member states against any threat of aggression. This commitment, embodied in Article 5 of the North Atlantic Treaty, should be reaffirmed in unmistakable terms. At the same time, NATO planners must recognize that the potential sources of Article 5 threats have broadened and now include dangers that could arise either inside or outside the Euro-Atlantic region. NATO must be prepared to defend against (and deter) such threats regardless of their point of origin.

There is, of course, nothing ambiguous about a cross border

military assault by the combined armed forces of a hostile country. However, there may well be doubts about whether an unconventional danger -- such as a cyber attack or evidence that terrorists are planning a strike -- triggers the collective defence mechanisms of Article 5. In the event, this will have to be determined by the NAC based on the nature, source, scope, and other aspects of the particular security challenge. For the purposes of planning, NATO should assume that serious threats will in fact materialize; preparations for detection, deterrence and response should be calibrated accordingly. These preparations, which should encompass adequate military capabilities, appropriate training exercises, information gathering, and strategic assessments, must correspond to the full range of potential Article 5 threats.

NATO's second core task should be to contribute to the broader security of the entire Euro-Atlantic region. Just as a homeowner has an interest in the safety of his or her neighbourhood, so NATO has reason to be concerned about stability throughout the region of which it is a part. Four decades ago, NATO's Harmel Report determined that "the ultimate political purpose of the Alliance is to achieve a just and lasting peaceful order in Europe accompanied by appropriate security guarantees." After the lifting of the Iron Curtain, NATO embraced the goal of building a Europe whole, free, and at peace. Over the past twenty years, leaders from both within and outside the Alliance have made extensive progress towards that objective. The kind of security that Western Europe has enjoyed for the past half century has been extended to Central and Eastern Europe. However, the job of constructing a fully stable order within Europe is not yet complete.

NATO operates as an important pillar of Euro-Atlantic security. In so doing, it functions neither in isolation from other organisations nor as a dominating force. The new Strategic Concept must identify NATO's appropriate role as a defender of its own interests and as a contributor to peace in every part of the region. The Alliance's close cooperation in the Balkans with the EU, the UN and the Organisation for Security and Co-operation in Europe (OSCE) is a prime example of how NATO can collaborate with other institutions in order to advance the wellbeing of people throughout the continent.

A number of elements come together in the performance of this core task, including NATO's partnerships with countries and organisations, and its support for -- and adherence to -- the principles that provide a framework for how governments in the region should act toward one another and toward their own citizens. These principles, which can be traced back to the Helsinki Accords (1975), find their present form in the Charter for European Security signed in Istanbul (1999). NATO also contributes to stability through its open door policy, which has provided important incentives within Europe for democracy, the peaceful settlement of disputes, and respect for human rights. In addition, NATO's diplomatic efforts with Russia,

Ukraine, Georgia and the other countries of the Caucasus, and other nonmember states show that nations do not have to be part of the Alliance to join with NATO on projects that benefit all.

NATO's third core task is to serve as a transatlantic means for security consultations and crisis management along the entire continuum of issues facing the Alliance. As the only contractual link between North America and Europe, NATO remains the essential venue for these functions and for fulfilling the common security and defence commitments of its members. This task reflects both the political and military dimensions of the Alliance and merits more attention in light of the diversity of today's security threats and the wide-ranging perspective of the organisation's current membership. After all, when the last Strategic Concept was written, the Alliance had far fewer members with shorelines on the Adriatic, Black and Baltic Seas.

The Alliance has an interest in protecting global lifelines that sustain modern societies and in promoting security and stability well beyond its immediate borders. That mission will in all likelihood be carried out in cooperation with its partners. Even though NATO's military tools are not always perfectly suited to address such challenges, Article 4 can provide a vital mechanism for identifying areas of common concern, devising an appropriate response, and coordinating NATO actions with partner organisations and states. To this end, the Alliance must further improve its crisis management capabilities, including the capacity to identify and to assess emerging risks, reassure member states, and undertake crisis response operations within, along, or beyond its borders.

Finally, as will become evident in the next chapter, the Group of Experts believes that enhancing the scope and management of partnerships has grown sufficiently important that it should be categorized as NATO's fourth core task, even though it represents less an end in itself than the means by which vital goals may be accomplished.

Chapter 3: Partnerships

Background

The passing years have created the need for a NATO of greater flexibility and reach, causing the

Alliance to turn more often to partners for help in responding to threats and in making the most effective use of its resources. Productive relationships with other countries and organisations enable NATO to be more vigilant, better prepared, and smarter in what it does. Although NATO's formal partnership arrangements began in Europe, they have since spread to encompass the Mediterranean and Middle East. In addition, some countries participate in NATO missions but do not fall within a formal partnership structure; these are categorized as operational partners.

In future missions, as now in Afghanistan, the Alliance may well function as one part of a broad network of security providers in which various international actors combine to take a comprehensive approach to the solution of a particular problem. This conception of teamwork should not be misunderstood. Some have interpreted the reference to "comprehensive" as a desire on NATO's part to assert a dominant global position or to put civilian organisations under military control. This is not the case: the comprehensive approach is not about hierarchy but about recognising that security has military, political, economic and social dimensions. It follows, therefore, that building security will often require working with an effective mix of partners to piece together the diverse elements of a single shared strategy. Depending on the specific circumstances, NATO will play either a leading or a complementary role. (Chapter five includes recommendations for improving NATO's capacity to contribute to a comprehensive approach.)

Analysis and Recommendations

NATO's first round of partnerships was aimed primarily at facilitating the entry of new members into the Alliance. A dozen new Allies later, that function has begun to diminish as other purposes have increased. A second generation of partnerships focused on adding capabilities for missions in such places as the Balkans and Afghanistan. A shift in thinking is needed now to obtain the maximum value from NATO's increasingly diverse and vital array of ties to organisations and governments. In this context, the NAC's recent decision to establish a single committee to manage all partnerships is a welcome one. The new Strategic Concept can help to guide that panel by recognizing that Alliance partnerships have diverse origins, serve varied purposes, and respond to different expectations. Each must be dealt with on its own terms; however, all have the potential to increase in value through continued adaptation and appropriate change.

Recommendation:

1. While strengthening organisational partnerships, NATO should examine whether its arrangements with countries and groups of countries can be improved by one or more of the following means:
   - Drafting a new or revised overall partnership agreement;

- Expanding the list of partnership activities;
- Allowing for greater differentiation among partners in their relationships with NATO;
- Introducing new agenda items, especially those that might lead to operational or diplomatic cooperation on specific projects; and
- Modifying procedures in order to encourage the freest possible exchange of ideas

Before recommending such measures, NATO should consult closely with all of the partners involved.

The Partnership for Peace (PfP) and the Euro-Atlantic Partnership Council (EAPC). The PfP and the

EAPC provide the framework for NATO's cooperation with partners in Europe and Eurasia. The former, established in 1994, has been the principal means for forging security links, while the EAPC was created several years later to provide a parallel political dialogue. Although the PfP is widely judged a success, the EAPC has not been used to its fullest potential. The Council was designed to enable NATO to conduct consultations with partner countries on political and security issues, but many participants complain that EAPC discussions are overly stilted and formal.

Recommendation:

1. NATO should strengthen routine and crisis consultations with EAPC partners as provided for under Paragraph 8

of the PfP framework
document.

Partnership with the EU. The EU
is a unique and essential partner to
NATO. The two institutions have a
largely overlapping membership, and
these common member states have
only one set of forces and one set of
taxpayers. Although NATO and the
EU have devised detailed
mechanisms for cooperation, these
have not always worked as well as
hoped. Still, expertise and
capabilities that countries develop
for the EU are frequently employed
in NATO missions and vice versa.
By definition, the 24 members have
shared interests and so work side-by-
side in virtually every theatre in
which NATO operates. Looking to
the past, the two institutions have
learned many of the same lessons;

looking to the future, they see a common set of problems.

Full complementarity between NATO and the EU will be essential if the Allies are to forge a comprehensive and cost-effective approach to security when both are involved in a stabilisation mission. Better cooperation can also be helpful in addressing unconventional threats such as terrorism, cyber-attacks, and energy vulnerabilities. The EU will often have more relevant expertise than NATO in countering the non-military aspects of such dangers, even though the line between military and non-military threats is becoming blurred. It should be noted, however, that full complementarity is only possible if non-EU NATO members and non-NATO EU members are accorded the same degree of transparency and involvement when joint activities are conducted.

Recommendations:

1. The new Strategic Concept should recognise that the EU's Treaty of Lisbon is designed, among other purposes, to strengthen Europe's military capabilities and command structures. Allies should welcome this development and use the Strategic Concept to affirm NATO's desire for a truly comprehensive partnership with the EU, one that is cost-effective, that is based on the principle of reciprocity and that encompasses the entire range of the institutions' mutual activities.

2. In its contacts with the EU, NATO leaders should avoid the

trap of categorising all threats and responsibilities as distinctly "military" or "non-military." Instead, they should nurture the habit of thinking of these issues as developing along a continuum. Many situations will require a response that includes both forceful and non-coercive elements; NATO, the EU, and others should bring to bear the capabilities that add the most value in finding a solution. Accordingly, NATO should seek to agree with EU leaders on a plan for regular joint participation in meetings, fuller communications between military staffs, and more extensive coordination with respect to crisis management, threat assessments, and sharing assets.

3. NATO and EU leaders should do everything possible to prevent disagreements from interfering with effective cooperation between the two organisations.

Partnership with the UN. NATO's partnership with the UN is also a central one due to the role played by that body within the world system and by the Allies' pledge of faith (invoked in the preamble to the North Atlantic Treaty) "in the purposes and principles of the Charter of the United Nations." The Security Council's mandate -- to safeguard international security and peace -- meshes well with the commitment of NATO members to "unite their efforts for collective defence and for the preservation of peace and security." It is clearly in NATO's interests to support the UN and to help strengthen its capacity to perform the many missions assigned to it by the global community.

NATO and the UN have worked together in a number of conflict zones, with the Alliance providing operational support and security so that the UN can move ahead on reconstruction, development, and governance-building. Although their partnership dates back more than a decade -- and while NATO and the UN signed a framework agreement in 2008 which has improved practical cooperation in some cases -- problems remain. UN personnel have been disappointed, on occasion, with the level of security and support that NATO provides. NATO tends to wait until a mission begins before starting to coordinate with the UN. When in theatre, the two institutions sometimes engage in disputes over their respective responsibilities.

Recommendations:

1. In a world of global threats, security depends increasingly on a rule-based international order. One of NATO's priorities, therefore, should be to strengthen the ability of the United Nations to fulfil its responsibilities.

2. When NATO and the UN are both operating in an area, the Alliance should do its best, if requested, to provide security for UN civilian personnel. Without a minimum level of security, the UN (and other NATO partners) will be unable to operate; without partners, NATO is often unable to meet its objectives. The earlier the need for coordination is

identified, the quicker joint planning can be done and the more likely it is that a mutually satisfactory security arrangement can be established.

3. NATO and the UN should improve their institutional links. A NATO liaison office at the UN would allow Alliance leaders to engage more easily with the Secretariat and with UN members. Additional forms of cooperation should be explored including participation in each other's training and exercise activities.

4. Coordination between the UN and NATO can prove crucial in the event of genocide, other massive violations of human rights, or humanitarian emergency. The Strategic Concept should make clear that

NATO is willing to consider requests from the UN to take appropriate action in such circumstances (possibly in support of other regional organisations), provided the NAC agrees to the mission and resources are available to carry it out.

5. NATO should work with the UN to respond positively to Security Council Resolution 1325, concerning the role of women in security and peace.

Partnership with the OSCE.
NATO's relationship with the OSCE is different and more intimate than it is with most other international organisations. NATO was a co-founder of the original Helsinki Process and played a significant role in lending substance to the OSCE's politico-military dimension. The

OSCE, in turn, is busy building democratic institutions in countries that do or may aspire to NATO membership, thus reinforcing NATO's own desire to encourage political stability and good governance in every corner of Europe.

Recommendations:

1. NATO should make full use of the OSCE's toolbox of training resources and expert advice in "soft security;" these are areas that can complement NATO's "hard security" tools.

2. The Alliance should actively pursue, under the framework of the OSCE, the negotiation of conventional arms control and confidence-building measures.

3. The Allies should also reflect on how the OSCE, a community rooted in

democratic values and freely accepted commitments, can complement NATO's own partnerships in building understanding of and support for the Alliance's activities.

Partnership with Russia. On the list of NATO partners, Russia is in its own category. The framework for partnership was spelled out in the 1997 Founding Act and the 2002 Declaration signed in Rome. Both documents express a commitment to identify and to pursue opportunities for joint action based on mutual interests and the understanding that security in the Euro-Atlantic region is indivisible. Cooperation is pledged in, among other areas, counter-terrorism, crisis management, arms control and non-proliferation, theatre missile defence, and responding to new threats. The NATO-Russia

Council (NRC) provides the forum for consultation, transparency, consensus-building, and making and implementing decisions.

NATO members, when asked, may vary in their descriptions of Russia while still seeing eye to eye on their prescriptions for engagement with that country. For reasons of history, geography, and recent events, some countries are more sceptical than others about the Russian government's commitment to a positive relationship. The fact that the NRC was not used to prevent the 2008 crisis in Georgia is unsettling, as is Moscow's oft-expressed wariness about NATO's intentions. Russia has sent conflicting signals about its openness to further cooperation with NATO, and its proposals for an alternative security order in Europe seem designed in part to constrain NATO's activities.

Although NATO members view Russia from diverse perspectives, the Alliance is united in its desire to engage with the leaders of that country in order to prevent harmful misunderstandings and to identify and to pursue shared goals. The Alliance does not consider any country to be its enemy; however, no one should doubt NATO's resolve if the security of any of its member states were to be threatened.

The fact that NATO is a defensive Alliance and that Russia's 2010 military doctrine is characterized by its authors as "strictly defensive" in nature provides a good starting point for cooperation. So, too, does the NATO-Russia joint commitment, expressed in the Founding Act, to create "in Europe a common space of security and stability, without dividing lines and spheres of influence limiting the sovereignty of any state."

Recommendations:

1. The new Strategic Concept should endorse a policy that combines reassurance for all Alliance members and constructive re-engagement with Russia.
2. The Strategic Concept should underscore NATO's desire for a qualitatively better relationship with Russia based on shared interests, mutual confidence, transparency and predictability. From the Alliance's perspective, the door to cooperation at all levels is and will remain open.
3. The Allies should work with Russia to ensure an agenda for

the NRC that responds in a frank and forward-looking way to the security concerns of both sides, and that identifies specific areas for joint action. The currently ongoing assessment of common threats and challenges is a helpful step. The two sides should also strive to enhance cooperation under the 2008 NRC Action Plan on Terrorism and to coordinate with other regional organisations.

Partnership with Georgia and Ukraine. Georgia and Ukraine have tailored partnership structures in the form of the NATO-Ukraine and NATO-Georgia Commissions. Channels of communication are excellent and both countries have contributed as partners to NATO missions. For geographic reasons, the two are touched by issues of longstanding regional concern including ethnic disputes and energy insecurity. One of the major failures of NATO's partnership structure was the 2008 conflict between Russia and Georgia, in which two Alliance partners engaged in hostilities over issues that remain unresolved.

Recommendations:

1. The Allies should make regular use of the NATO-Ukraine and NATO-Georgia commissions to discuss mutual security concerns and to foster practical cooperation, including on defence reforms. The clearer NATO articulates its position to the partners and the more accurately it can assess their perceptions, the more adept the Allies will be at defusing crises and building trust.

2. The Allies should also employ NATO's crisis management mechanisms, in association with the partnership commissions, to assess and monitor security developments affecting these two countries.

NATO's Partnerships in the Mediterranean and Middle East. The area encompassing North Africa and the Middle East has long been among the globe's most strategically important regions. Its future development will affect NATO's interests in nuclear non-proliferation, counter-terrorism, energy security and a peaceful international order. In light of these interests, the Alliance is engaged in this vast and varied region through the Mediterranean Dialogue (MD) and the more recent Istanbul Cooperation Initiative (ICI).

Mediterranean Dialogue. Begun in 1994, the MD includes seven nations from the Mediterranean region. The Dialogue provides a framework for confidence building, transparency and cooperation. Although it is the only functioning region-wide security initiative, its accomplishments to date are modest. The Dialogue lacks a founding document of the type developed for other NATO partnerships. Potential areas of common interest include weapons proliferation and missile defence. The present MD formula remains workable, but should be flexible enough to allow any country that desires to deepen its partnership with NATO to do so.

NATO is strongly supportive of efforts to negotiate a just and lasting peace between Israelis and Palestinians, but does not play an active diplomatic role. The Alliance has, however, expressed a willingness to assist in implementing an agreement should one be reached, provided that is requested by the parties and authorized by the UN Security Council.

Istanbul Cooperation Initiative. The ICI, launched in 2004, aims to contribute to long term global and regional security by offering countries in the broader Middle East bilateral security cooperation with NATO. The initiative is open to all countries in the region who support its goals, including the fight against terrorism and the proliferation of weapons of mass destruction. Although potentially valuable, the ICI has been held back by a lack of common strategic vision and by rivalries among the partners and some Allies. Nonetheless, like the

MD, the ICI is helping to build needed security relationships and to open channels for regular dialogue. Each partnership is also an instrument for changing perceptions, which is helpful because populations in the region are not always fully or fairly informed about either NATO or the West more generally.

Recommendations:

1. NATO should approach its relations with countries in the Mediterranean and Middle East with strategic patience. The MD and ICI are still relatively new and the political discussion and practical cooperation they provide can enhancemutual understanding, contribute to stability, and improve NATO's image in the region. One way to increase the mutual value of the MD and

ICI to the Alliance might be to pursue an agreed statement of shared interests based on new and broader concepts of security, taking into account conventional and unconventional dangers, as well as political, economic, social and cultural issues.

2. The Allies should be open to transparent consultations with its MD and ICI partners on the implications of a possible nuclear breakout by Iran.

3. NATO should be ready to assist in implementing a peace agreement between Israel and the Palestinians consistent with the conditions that have been established

Partners Across the Globe. NATO now has important operational partners from outside the Euro-

Atlantic area, some of whom have been key contributors to Allied missions. Australia, in fact, contributes more troops to Afghanistan than half the NATO Allies, New Zealand is also a significant contributor, the Republic of Korea has pledged to deploy a sizable contingent, and Japan has committed billions of dollars to the reconstruction efforts there. These democracies are not only partners of need, but also partners of values -- even though they do not participate within a formal framework for dialogue such as that provided by the EAPC. Afghanistan and Pakistan, whose cooperation is crucial to the success of the International Security Assistance Force (ISAF) are also outside any formal structure for dialogue with NATO.

NATO does not necessarily require a formal partnership in order to maintain a productive working dialogue with other countries and organisations. It does need to maintain an active diplomatic presence in order to take advantage of opportunities for collaboration when they arise. For example, the People's Republic of China has participated alongside units from Allied countries in the course of UN peace operations and in anti-piracy patrols around the Gulf of Aden. Countries in Central and South Asia have a major stake in maintaining stability in their region. Members of the Collective Security Treaty Organisation and the Shanghai Cooperation Organisation have shown an interest in working cooperatively with other multinational entities. India, Indonesia, and the leading democracies of Africa and Latin America share with NATO a commitment to global peace and the rule of law

Recommendations:

1. NATO should do more to deepen its partnerships with countries outside the Euro-Atlantic region by expanding the list of shared activities while preserving the ability of individual partners to form tailored co-operative relationships with the Alliance.

2. The Allies agreed in Istanbul in 2004 to expand the access of operational partners to information and planning and has since made some progress in this regard. The Strategic Concept should go further and outline ways to give NATO's operational partners a regular

and meaningful voice in shaping strategy and decisions on missions to which they contribute.

3. NATO should explore the possibility of new regional subgroups if there is interest among countries in doing so. Another, and perhaps preferable, alternative is for NATO to forge more formal ties to such bodies as the African Union, the Organization of American States, the Gulf Cooperation Council, the Shanghai Cooperation Organisation, or the Collective Security Treaty Organisation. Any such relationship should be based on the principles of equality, mutual trust, and mutual benefit.

Chapter 4: Political and Organisational Issues

Background

Since 1999, the Alliance has almost doubled in size, confronted a number of new dangers, engaged in operations more distant and complex than any previously attempted, lived through a severe international economic crisis, and established political dialogues and partnerships that extend far beyond the Euro-Atlantic region. Not surprisingly, these rapid changes have been accompanied by considerable internal strain. The new Strategic Concept allows the Alliance to take stock of recent events and to search for a fresh consensus on issues that are central to the future management and direction of the organisation. These issues include:

- Lessons of Afghanistan
- Guidelines for missions outside Alliance borders
- Administrative reforms
- Decision-making procedures
- Open Door Policy
- NATO's role in conventional arms control

Analysis and Recommendations

Lessons of Afghanistan. NATO assumed leadership of ISAF in August 2003. Since then, the operation has grown from 5000 to roughly 100,000 troops, coming from forty-six countries, including all NATO members. Its mission is to assist the Afghan Government in exercising and extending its authority for the purpose of stabilizing the country and fostering peaceful reconstruction and development. To these ends, it carries out military operations and helps to train and assist the Afghan National Army and Police. Although ISAF has achieved much, its experience has led to concerns within the Alliance about unity of command, restrictions (or caveats) placed on the troops contributed by some Allies, and questions about tactics and goals. The mission has also suffered setbacks due to incidents involving civilian casualties, which NATO commanders have pledged to minimize.

ISAF is, because of its size and duration, an extraordinary operation. It was also unanticipated. In light of the complex and unpredictable security climate likely to prevail through the coming decade, it is not possible to rule out NATO's future participation in similar (although hopefully less extended) stabilisation missions. The experience in Afghanistan thus provides for NATO a valuable list of lessons learned. Many of the principles that should be included in the new Strategic Concept are present. Most obvious is the importance of being able to deploy military units tailored to specific and sustained operations at a distance from Alliance borders. Other lessons include:

- To the maximum feasible extent, NATO's military forces should operate under a unified chain of command.
- Allies should minimize the national caveats that they attach when contributing troops to Alliance operations; any caveats that are imposed should be clearly and explicitly stated and their impact carefully

evaluated during force generation and operational planning.

- NATO's mission in Afghanistan has been damaged in the past by its failure to communicate its intentions clearly and by incidents and accidents involving civilian casualties. Recent restrictions on close air support and artillery fire implemented by the ISAF Commander are helping to reduce this problem, but the need to shield civilians must continue to be stressed in training and in the field.
- Prisoners and detainees should be treated in accordance with the principles of international law. Any other policy leads to unfavourable political consequences, loss of moral credibility, harm to Alliance

cohesion, and increased danger to NATO forces.

- Stability in Afghanistan will not come through military means alone. As in other counter-insurgency situations, a primary objective is to create a comprehensive civilian-military approach that enables the local governing structure to earn the trust and loyalty of the local population. For NATO, this requires the ability to work closely with partner organisations to align priorities and to make the best possible use of available resources. It also places a premium on helping host nation security forces to improve their own ability to maintain order and to protect non-combatants from harm.

Guidelines for Missions Outside Alliance Borders. For all its assets, NATO is by no means the sole answer to every problem affecting international security. NATO is a regional, not a global organisation; its financial resources are limited and subject to other priorities; and it has no desire to take on missions that other institutions and countries can be counted upon to handle. Accordingly, the new Strategic Concept should prescribe guidelines for the Alliance as it makes decisions about when and where to apply resources beyond its borders. Because every situation is unique, NATO decision-making can only be made on a case-by-case basis. However, deliberations within the NAC should give weight to such factors as:

- the extent and imminence of danger to Alliance members;
- the exhaustion or apparent ineffectiveness of alternative steps;
- the ability and willingness of NATO members to provide the means required for success;
- the involvement of partners in helping to ensure an effective and timely remedy to the problem at hand;
- the collateral impact on other NATO missions and needs;
- the degree of domestic and international public support;
- conformity with international law; and
- the foreseeable consequences of inaction.

In the future as in the past, NATO leaders should bear in mind two cautions: NATO's commitments should never exceed what the Alliance can do; but what NATO can do should never be outpaced by NATO's security needs. The Alliance cannot be so ambitious that it takes on jobs that it is unprepared to perform, but neither can it be so lethargic that it fails to prepare itself for necessary tasks.

Accordingly, the Strategic Concept should include a clear statement of defence priorities. These begin with the ability to defend Alliance territory, but include the capacity to undertake demanding missions at strategic distance, help shape the international security landscape, and respond to unpredictable contingencies when and where that is required. NATO's official Level of Ambition was set out in 2006; there is no need to modify those benchmarks, although the definition of mission could be broadened to include new requirements for homeland security, including cyber security.

It is a truism that NATO cannot succeed without the support of its members. Similarly, NATO missions will not go well for long unless they are understood and embraced by the populations of NATO countries. Such backing cannot be taken for granted. The more open NATO leaders are in their deliberations, and the more clearly they explain the specific goals and rationale for NATO participation in any operation, the more likely it is that the Alliance will be able to attract the level of popular and parliamentary support it must have to fulfil its missions.

Recommendations:

1. The Strategic Concept should include a set of guidelines for informing NATO decision-making with respect to undertaking new missions or responsibilities.
2. NATO should maintain a level of preparedness and operational tempo that responds to the security needs of its members, thus avoiding the danger of over-reach on one extreme and complacency on the other.
3. Through transparency and effective public communications, the Alliance must strive to attract and maintain public and legislative backing for its operations.

Administrative Reforms. As NATO has grown, so has its structure, including the number of its committees, the size of its staff, and the cost of doing routine business. The Secretary General has identified internal reform as a priority and Allies have given him a clear mandate to act.

Recommendations:

1. The Strategic Concept should endorse a far-reaching agenda of reforms. This agenda should include -- but not be restricted to -- streamlining the international Secretariat, reviewing financial rules, reducing headquarters operating costs, and shrinking the number of committees and agencies.
2. The Secretary General should have added authority to implement his reform agenda.
3. The Allies should establish quantitative targets for savings

in various categories of administrative costs and should ensure that savings realized through the reform process are reinvested in NATO's readiness and operational capabilities.

Decision-making procedures.

There is an inherent tension between a multimember organisation that works by consensus and a military/political Alliance operating in a fluid and fast-paced security environment. This tension has not been diminished by NATO's larger membership or by the proliferation of its committees. In 2009, the Secretary General put forward some initial ideas for streamlining the decision-making process. The challenge for Alliance leaders will be to identify further steps that do not, in themselves, become a source of division. The consensus rule has always been a fundamental principle in NATO and Allies are strongly attached to its preservation. However, the need to achieve agreement among twenty-eight states (and more in the future) can prove arduous, sometimes leading to delays that serve no constructive purpose. In addition, the Alliance needs to prepare for situations where rapid (indeed almost instantaneous) decision-making may be required.

Recommendations:

1. In his proposals for administrative reform, the Secretary General is encouraged to include further proposals for streamlining the decision-making process. These proposals should: 1) recognize that any departure from the consensus principle

must be approved by the NAC; 2) preserve the consensus rule for the most important decisions such as those involving Article 5 commitments, budgets, new missions, or new members; 3) identify means on less vital questions for Allies to register concerns short of a veto; and 4) establish the principle that the implementation of decisions arrived at by consensus should not be delayed by efforts to review those decisions at lower levels before they are carried out.

2. The Alliance should consider giving the Secretary General or NATO military leaders certain pre-delegated authorities, based on agreed rules of engagement, to respond in an emergency

situation such as a missile or cyber attack.

Open Door Policy. Since its founding in 1949, NATO has increased in size from a dozen members to twenty-eight. This open door policy was authorized by Article 10 of the North Atlantic Treaty which provides that the "Parties may, by unanimous agreement, invite any other European State in a position to further the principles of this Treaty and to contribute to the security of the North Atlantic area to accede" to membership in the Alliance. Since 1995, the process of enlargement has been guided by certain principles, including the following:

- Democratic values and full support for NATO's political vision within the candidate country;

- The implementation of any necessary military reforms in order to achieve NATO standards with respect to professionalism and to ensure civilian control over the armed forces;
- The fair treatment of minority populations;
- The peaceful resolution of domestic and international disputes;
- Domestic political support for NATO membership; and
- The overall ability of the candidate to contribute to the security of the Alliance and the Euro-Atlantic region.

Recommendation:

1. The new Strategic Concept should reaffirm NATO's open door policy, including the principles listed above.

NATO's role in conventional arms control policy. NATO members have a major stake in arms control, but the Alliance as an entity has only a limited formal role. In the past, it has debated developments with a particular impact on European security, such as the Intermediate-Range Nuclear Forces Treaty of 1987 (even though actual negotiations were conducted bilaterally between the United States and the Soviet Union). More significantly, the Allies were directly involved in negotiating and signing the 1990 Treaty on Conventional Armed Forces in Europe (CFE).

In recent years, the CFE process has stalled and is now in danger of crumbling. This is regrettable because the CFE has led in the past to the destruction of tens of thousands of tanks, armoured vehicles, and artillery pieces, while increasing predictability and transparency throughout the region.

Recommendation:

1. The Strategic Concept should underline NATO's commitment to a robust and stabilizing conventional arms control regime in Europe, based on the principles of mutual transparency, restraint, and host-nation consent for the stationing of foreign forces. With this goal in mind, the Alliance should support the revival of the CFE process and express a willingness to engage in constructive dialogue with all CFE states.

Chapter 5: Alliance Forces and Capabilities

Background

NATO's 1999 Strategic Concept included a section on "Guidelines for the Alliance's Forces" which established goals for transforming capabilities to meet the challenges of a new century. The document called for a well-trained and equipped force and command structure able to provide collective defence, respond rapidly to emergencies, and engage in complex joint operations beyond Allied territory. At the same summit in Washington, leaders approved a separate Defence Capabilities Initiative (DCI) to address five broad NATO force needs: 1) Mobility and Deployability, 2) Sustainability and Logistics, 3) Effective Engagement, 4) Survivability, and 5) Interoperable

Communications. Although necessary and timely, the DCI also proved to be too broad in focus. Over the next decade, subsequent capabilities initiatives and summit declarations provided additional guidance to NATO members and defence planners.

Guidance in the past decade. At its 2002 summit in Prague, Allies began to adapt to the changed security situation generated by the 9/11 attacks and to the prospect of helping to restore stability to Afghanistan. The Alliance approved a plan to augment the DCI by developing improved capabilities in eight defence categories, established Allied Command Transformation (ACT) to steer the development of those capabilities, and created a NATO Response Force (NRF) to "move [forces] quickly to wherever needed."

At the Riga summit in 2006, Alliance leaders adopted the Comprehensive Political Guidance (CPG), which set out the framework and priorities for all Alliance capability issues, planning disciplines, and intelligence for the foreseeable future. Among its requirements was that NATO members develop national land forces that were at least 40 percent deployable and 8 percent deployable on a sustainable basis. (These targets were later raised to 50 percent and 10 percent.)

In 2009, at the Strasbourg-Kehl summit, NATO agreed to a "Declaration of Alliance Security," which emphasised implementation of the CPG and envisioned a

multinational headquarters for
special operations forces.

**Military transformation: a work in
progress.** The results of these
initiatives and summit directives
have been mixed. Due in the main to
limited resources, NATO's military
forces have moved only slowly to
pursue agreed guidelines. Thus, a
significant distance still separates
potential missions and available
capabilities. Much of the progress
that has taken place towards military
transformation has been driven by
operational requirements in Kosovo
and Afghanistan. ISAF operations in
particular have underlined the need
for forces that are deployable and
sustainable, for common approaches
to counter-insurgency operations,
and for interoperable command,
control, communications, computers,

intelligence, surveillance and reconnaissance (C4ISR) capabilities.

The primary limiting factor hindering military transformation has been the lack of European defence spending and investment. Today, only six of twenty-six European Allies spend 2 percent or more of GDP on these purposes; only about a dozen have met goals for making military forces deployable and sustainable. The Alliance benchmark of 20 percent of military spending allocated to investment has been achieved by less than half of NATO nations (though the trend is slowly improving). The gap is especially large between U.S. capabilities and the rest of NATO, an imbalance that if left unchecked could undermine Alliance cohesion. Contributing to the problem is the fact that, in the past twenty years, European defence spending has been consumed disproportionately by personnel and operational costs. As a result, European national forces generally do not have nearly enough transformed forces.

Analysis and Recommendations

The new Strategic Concept should provide direction for the further transformation of NATO's defence capabilities. Given the nature of the modern security environment and constraints on fiscal resources, NATO will need a flexible, deployable, networked, and sustainable military force posture that can meet the full range of Alliance responsibilities at an affordable cost. These responsibilities include the deterrence of aggression, the defence of Alliance territory, undertaking demanding missions at strategic distance, and preparing for a wide range of lesser contingencies. The new Strategic Concept should update the guidelines established in the 1999 Concept and be accompanied by an agreed set of priority capabilities and military reforms to be endorsed by Alliance leaders at the Lisbon Summit.

NATO's Military Missions. In the coming decade, NATO will have four central interrelated military missions; these missions will complement the core tasks outlined in Chapter Two. They are:

- Deter, prevent and defend against any threat of aggression in order to ensure the political independence and territorial integrity of every NATO member in accordance with

Article 5 of the North Atlantic
Treaty.

- Cooperate with partners and
  civilian institutions to protect
  the treaty area against a full
  range of unconventional
  security challenges.

- Deploy and sustain
  expeditionary capabilities for
  military operations beyond the
  treaty area when required to
  prevent an attack on the treaty
  area or to protect the legal
  rights and other vital interests
  of Alliance members.

- Help to shape a more stable
  and peaceful international
  security environment by
  enhancing partner
  interoperability, providing
  military and police training,
  coordinating military
  assistance, and cooperating

with the governments of key countries.

Conventional Defence Capabilities. If NATO is to fulfil these four missions successfully, it must halt the precipitous decline in national defence spending, implement new reforms and efficiencies, and set priorities for future capabilities. Important steps need to be taken at the Lisbon summit on all three counts. The Secretary General has already undertaken significant reform efforts; these are well worthy of encouragement and support. In addition, prior to Lisbon, clear priorities for capabilities requirements need to be prepared for approval by Alliance leaders. Defence priorities include those related to Article 5 needs and to the goal of military transformation.

Recommendation:

1. The new Strategic Concept should address, in addition to other priorities, the following conventional defence needs:

- *Provide reassurance on Article 5 commitment.* Assuring Allies with regard to Article 5 requires refreshing and maintaining essential skills and capabilities. The Alliance has developed adequate military readiness criteria to meet Article 5 commitments but it should do more to guarantee its readiness in practice. This will require better contingency planning, preparations for crisis management, equipment assessments, and appropriate military exercises. Such exercises should not be provocative, should be announced in advance, and should be open to observers from neighbouring countries.

- *Achieve deployability and sustainability goals.* Forces offered to NATO by members or partners for any mission within or beyond NATO territory should be both deployable and sustainable. To this end, Allies should restructure more of their forces away from traditional fixed territorial defence missions. Deployability also requires strategic lift, which is in short supply, although the C-17 consortium is a step in the right direction. Creating a NATO Deployment Agency is an idea that has merit and should be explored. Such an agency could take responsibility for consolidating all aspects of

Alliance preparations for rapid deployment.

- *Broaden the role of the NATO Response Force.* The NRF should be prepared to undertake Article 5 as well as non-Article 5 missions and should be a central participant when Article 5 exercises are conducted.

- *Capitalize on commonality between Article 5 and expeditionary missions.* NATO needs to be prepared for both Article 5 and non-Article 5 missions. To achieve both goals efficiently, it should review the two mission sets -- which are neither entirely identical nor wholly different -- for areas of commonality. The core similarity is that both missions require well-prepared forces and support assets. The core difference is that a major combat operation in Europe against a serious adversary is inherently different from involvement by an expeditionary force in a stabilisation operation in a distant state. To be ready for both, NATO must take full advantage of overlaps between the two.

- *Understand C4ISR as NATO's operational glue.* C4ISR capabilities provide the operational sinew binding NATO and national forces together into an interoperable, agile, and cohesive whole. They should be a high priority for future investment by members as well as by NATO itself. Allies should invest first in compliance with the latest NATO CIS architectures and

ISR platform standards.
Likewise, NATO should ensure
the same architectural
standards are met and
maintained across its command
structure. Allies and partners
should emphasise investment
in national systems at the
tactical and operational levels
that will tie into NATO's
strategic-operational networks.

- *Strengthen Special Operations
  Forces (SOF) capabilities.*
  Much has already been done to
  bring together the SOF
  capabilities of members and
  partners, including the
  establishment of the NATO
  Special Operations
  Headquarters. This body is
  developing common training
  and doctrine as well as
  enhancing intelligence sharing.
  More can be done to sharpen

NATO's ability to make use of these expeditionary capabilities. In keeping with the Strasbourg-Kehl Summit Declaration, the NAC should consider designating NATO Special Operations Headquarters as a full component command.

- *Upgrade Allied Command Transformation.* ACT needs a bolder mandate, greater authorities, and more resources. It should champion the development of both transformational capabilities and new efficiency measures. It should also take full charge of NATO lessons learned, doctrine, training and education programmes.
- *Transform NATO Education and Training.* Led by ACT, NATO should exploit the

information revolution by establishing a process of continual learning for military and civilian personnel. People are NATO's foremost asset and up-to-date knowledge is an essential attribute for its people. Modern educational tools, including distance learning, exchanges, and emergency simulations can burnish operational and strategic skills. To the extent possible, these programmes should include personnel from partner countries and organisations.

- *Enhance maritime situational awareness.* A new level of secure maritime situational awareness is called for by changing risks around the periphery of NATO and in the High North, Gulf, Indian

Ocean and other areas. NATO should harmonize investments in such surveillance platforms as unmanned aerial vehicles, maritime patrol aircraft, land-based radars, surface and subsurface vessels, and robotic systems. NATO should also agree on specific surveillance mission areas that underpin Article 5, such as those related to illegal attacks on shipping, WMD proliferation and terrorist activities.

Reforms and efficiencies. If NATO is to keep pace with evolving threats, it must improve its capabilities more rapidly than it has. The challenge of catching up is aggravated by a less than favourable economic climate. The best and most realistic way to close the gap is through a commitment to efficiency measures and other reforms. The economic and military logic behind such reforms is clear, yet nations may still be reluctant to undertake them. Leadership is required.

Recommendation:

1. A balanced package of reform and efficiency proposals should be developed by the Secretary General in time for presentation to the heads of government at the Lisbon summit. As part of this package, NATO should encourage:

   o new, truly multinational formations with unified command and control, interdependent logistics and integrated civilian-military components;

- new informal pooling arrangements, especially for lift;
- increased NATO common funding and interoperability for C4ISR;
- common approaches to logistics;
- the further evolution and coordination of national specialisation and niche capabilities;
- exploration of opportunities for additional multinational procurement programs;
- development of a NATO/EU defence capabilities agency;
- using common funds for costs related to selected deployments, including

an annual exercise of the NRF; and

o a further review of NATO's command structure for the purpose of reducing costs and enhancing force flexibility and deployability.

Comprehensive approach. Several years after the concept of a comprehensive approach was widely accepted as the best means for responding to complex security challenges, NATO efforts to operate with civilian partners remain disjointed. As noted earlier, such an approach often requires NATO to act in partnership with other organisations, whether in a leading or a supportive role. The Alliance's 2006 CPG describes NATO's approach to conflicts as "the coherent and comprehensive application of the various instruments of the Alliance to create overall effects that will achieve the desired outcome." The CPG also states that NATO has "no requirement to develop capabilities strictly for civilian purposes," relying instead on its partners. Although true in theory, this logic has not always proven out in practice. Effective military-civilian relationships require a good deal of hard work. Military and civilian personnel tend to plan differently, set different priorities, establish different standards of accountability, recruit and deploy personnel differently, and often even speak the same language in ways that one has trouble understanding the other. In fact, NATO today does not work as well as it should -- indeed, as it must -- with civilian organisations. The

Strategic Concept must address this shortcoming, while also encouraging each Ally to improve the ability of its military to work with civilian partners.

Recommendations:

1. NATO at all levels should prepare to be part of integrated civilian-military missions. This requires establishing a small civilian planning unit within NATO to maintain points of contact, share information, and engage in joint planning with partner countries and organisations.

2. NATO should maintain up-to-date memoranda of understanding with such key institutions as the UN, the EU and the OSCE, as well as other national and regional bodies and major NGOs.

3. NATO's Defence Planning Process should identify civilian capabilities -- whether NATO or non-NATO -- to be deployed along with initial combat forces for immediate post-conflict stability operations.

4. NATO should ask member states to identify a cadre of civilian specialists with experience in complex operations who would be available for rapid deployment for selected missions if qualified personnel from partner countries or institutions are not. These civilian reservists should be prepared through NATO training to move into an area in the wake of conflict and to work with local authorities and combat forces for a limited period of

time in order to provide security and other public services.

5. NATO should strive on a systematic basis to help potential partners improve their ability to contain and respond to crisis situations; this can be done through -- among other means -- training, material assistance, and strategic assessments aimed at early warning and prevention.

Nuclear Weapons and Arms Control. NATO relies upon a mixture of conventional and nuclear weapons for the purpose of deterring an armed attack. Changes in threats to the Alliance have broadened the concept of deterrence and allowed NATO to dramatically reduce the types, numbers and roles of its nuclear forces. At the same time, global leaders -- including many from Allied nations -- have expressed a desire to move toward a world free from the threat posed by nuclear arms. Looking ahead, the Alliance should be prepared for in-depth consultations on the future role of nuclear weapons in its deterrence strategy. Some parameters for those consultations, which will take place against the backdrop of the larger global nuclear debate, are suggested below:

- As long as nuclear weapons remain a reality in international relations, the Alliance should retain a nuclear component to its deterrent strategy -- at the minimum level required by the prevailing security environment.
- Under current security conditions, the retention of

some U.S. forward-deployed systems on European soil reinforces the principle of extended nuclear deterrence and collective defence.

- Broad participation of the non-nuclear Allies is an essential sign of transatlantic solidarity and risk sharing. Participation by the non-nuclear states can take place in the form of nuclear deployments on their territory or by non-nuclear support measures.

- NATO should continue to ensure the absolute physical security of nuclear weapons stored on European soil.

- There should be an ongoing NATO dialogue with Russia on nuclear perceptions, concepts, doctrines, and transparency. These talks should help set the stage for the further reduction and possible eventual elimination of the entire class of sub-strategic nuclear weapons.

- NATO should re-establish the Special Consultative Group on Arms Control for the purpose of facilitating its own internal dialogue about the whole range of issues related to nuclear doctrine, new arms control initiatives, and proliferation.
- NATO should make clear its full support for efforts to prevent the proliferation of nuclear weapons, to reduce further the prominence of nuclear arms in the defence doctrines of any country, and to ensure that nuclear materials are handled in a safe and secure manner.
- NATO should endorse a policy of not using or threatening to

use nuclear weapons against non-nuclear states that are party to the Nuclear Non-Proliferation Treaty and in compliance with their nuclear non-proliferation obligations.

Recommendation:

1. As long as nuclear weapons exist, NATO should continue to maintain secure and reliable nuclear forces, with widely shared responsibility for deployment and operational support, at the minimum level required by the prevailing security environment. Any change in this policy, including in the geographic distribution of NATO nuclear deployments in Europe, should be made, as with other major decisions, by the Alliance as a whole.

2. NATO should invite an ongoing dialogue with Russia on nuclear perceptions, concepts, doctrines, and transparency, and should convene a Special Consultative Group in order to inform and coordinate its internal dialogue about nuclear-related issues.

Ballistic missile defence. The Alliance should have a fuller role in dealing with the emerging ballistic missile threat. The new U.S. phased, adaptive approach to ballistic missile defence provides an opportunity for the development of an effective NATOwide strategy that would add to the defence of populations as well as forces. The U.S. systems to be deployed will be much more effective against the ballistic missile threat to Europe from the Gulf than those previously envisioned. They are not directed against Russia, nor would they threaten Russia's nuclear deterrent. A NATO missile defence system would enhance deterrence and transatlantic sharing of responsibility, reinforce the principle that security is indivisible, and allow for concrete security cooperation with Russia.

Recommendation:

1. NATO should recognize territorial missile defence as an essential mission of the Alliance. To that end, NATO should agree to expand its Active Layered Theatre Ballistic Missile Defence System to provide the core command and control capability of a NATO territorial missile defence system.

Responding to Unconventional Dangers. Throughout the Group's investigation, NATO's response to terrorism, cyber vulnerabilities, energy security, and climate change was discussed. Some new capabilities may be needed.

Strengthening NATO's role in fighting terrorism. NATO's military forces are playing a vital role in the fight against violent extremism in Afghanistan. Within the treaty area, however, counter-terrorism is primarily the responsibility of police and other domestic agencies. Nonetheless, the Alliance can play a supporting part through the protection of vital military facilities, sharing intelligence, and providing assistance, when asked, in consequence management. It is worth recalling, for example, that NATO aircraft flew AWACS patrols over the United States for seven months following the 9/11 attacks. In 2004, the Alliance established a Defence Against Terrorism Programme that was designed to develop new technologies to protect troops and civilians against such dangers as improvised explosive devices, suicide bombs and anti-aircraft rocket strikes.

Recommendation:

1. NATO's Defence Against Terrorism Programme should expand from its current focus on ten areas of technology-related work to include, among other subjects, collaborative research on investigative techniques, deterrence, and social networking.

Cyber defence capabilities. The next significant attack on the Alliance

may well come down a fibre optic
cable. Already, cyber attacks against
NATO systems occur frequently, but
most often below the threshold of
political concern. However, the risk
of a large-scale attack on NATO's
command and control systems or
energy grids could readily warrant
consultations under Article 4 and
could possibly lead to collective
defence measures under Article 5.
Effective cyber defence requires the
means to prevent, detect, respond to,
and recover from attacks. NATO has
taken steps to develop these
capabilities through creation of a
Cyber Defence Management
Authority, a Cooperative Cyber
Defence Centre of Excellence, and a
Computer Incident Response
Capability. Nonetheless, there persist
serious gaps in NATO's cyber
defence capabilities. The Strategic
Concept should place a high priority

on addressing these vulnerabilities, which are both unacceptable and increasingly dangerous.

Recommendation:

1. NATO should recognize that cyber attacks are a growing threat to the security of the Alliance and its members. Accordingly:
    - A major effort should be undertaken to increase the monitoring of NATO's critical network and to assess and furnish remedies to any vulnerabilities that are identified.
    - The Centre of Excellence should do more, through training, to help members improve their cyber defence programmes.

- o Allies should expand early warning capabilities in the form of a NATO-wide network of monitoring nodes and sensors.
- o The Alliance should be prepared to send an expert team to any member experiencing or threatened by a major cyber attack.
- o Over time, NATO should plan to mount a fully adequate array of cyber defence capabilities, including passive and active elements.

Energy security. Access to sufficient supplies of energy is a requirement for any modern state. However, most countries are dependent, to one degree or another, on external energy sources and on the means for delivering needed supplies via pipelines or shipping. Any substantial or sudden interruption of supplies to an Ally would be of concern, especially if the interruption were caused by the sabotage of energy infrastructure or by unlawful interference with maritime commerce. Such an occurrence, if prolonged, could lead to consultations under Article 4 of the North Atlantic Treaty and to a determination by the Allies of an appropriate response.

As a general matter, energy policy is a domestic issue, with the EU and the International Energy Agency offering services at the multinational level related to potential energy supply disruptions. NATO, however, has an obligation to protect its own energy reserves in order to ensure the capability of its forces. Also, in 2008 the Alliance agreed at the Bucharest Summit to take a number of additional steps pertaining to energy security, including the sharing of intelligence, support for the protection of critical infrastructure, and support for an expanded dialogue with energy supplier countries.

Recommendation:

1. The potential for major energy supply disruptions should figure prominently in NATO's strategic assessment and contingency planning activities. Thought should be given in advance to how the Alliance might work with partners in an emergency situation to mitigate harm to its members and to find alternative sources of supply.

Climate change. As an Alliance, NATO does not have a formal role in regulating the greenhouse gas emissions that experts believe lead to global warming. NATO could, however, be called upon to help cope with security challenges stemming from such consequences of climate change as a melting polar ice cap or an increase in catastrophic storms and other natural disasters. The Alliance should keep this possibility in mind when preparing for future contingencies.

Chapter 6: Conclusion

The process of developing a new Strategic Concept should provide a timely reminder to all that NATO serves unique and indispensable functions. Without NATO during the Cold War, the Euro-Atlantic region would have entered the twenty-first century deprived of freedom in its East and with no common strategy in its West; the world would still be hostage to a superpower rivalry, with nuclear annihilation a single miscalculation away.

Without NATO in the 1990s, the newly-freed states of Central and East Europe would have lacked a powerful incentive to embrace democracy internally and to mend fences with external rivals. Meanwhile, the Balkans would have remained a cauldron of ethnic bitterness, ruled by the sword, and split asunder by the memory of past conflicts.

If NATO did not exist today, Afghanistan might once again be ruled by the Taliban, providing a safe haven for al-Qa'ida, allowing terrorists to train and to plan their attacks systematically and without fear. Euro-Atlantic states would lack an effective community forum for responding to traditional threats and emerging perils.

Without NATO in the future, the prospects for international stability and peace would be far more uncertain than they are. The Alliance is not alone in its commitment to these objectives, but its combination of military capability and political solidarity make it both singularly valuable and irreplaceable.

NATO thrives as a source of hope because, from the very beginning, its members have described their common agenda in a positive fashion: to enhance international security, safeguard liberty, and promote the rule of law. These objectives are neither tied to any calendar nor diminished by any advance in technology. They do not depend on any particular adversary. They are enduring needs and will survive as long as NATO has the courage to defend them through the unity of its members, the bravery of its citizens, and the free expression of its collective will.

NATO Afghan First Policy

Supporting Afghan Economic Development

1. Recognising the crucial link between maintaining stability and delivering development aid to Afghanistan, the NATO Heads of State and Government (HOSG) adopted at the Bucharest Summit *"a comprehensive approach across security, governance and development efforts and between all local and international partners"* in order to support Afghanistan's transition from conflict to stability, reconstruction and sustainable development. NATO HOSG also set out the growth of Afghanistan's licit economy as one of the strategic desired outcomes.

2. In implementation of this approach, the **NATO Afghan First Policy** is developed by the NATO

Economic Committee in coordination with the NATO Senior Resource Board, following an agreement by NATO Foreign Ministers in December 2009, to maximise, to the extent possible, the positive impact of ISAF presence in Afghanistan. It aims at strengthening NATO's contribution to the development of the Afghan economy by increasing local procurement of goods and services whenever the acceptable standards for security, quality, price and reliable supply are met; including the use of Afghan contractors and the employment of Afghan labour for works and jobs in Afghanistan.

Benefits of Procuring Afghan Goods and Services

3. Increasing local procurement in Afghanistan is considered the most

important step in promoting the development of the Afghan private sector and supporting the economic development of the country. The analysis undertaken by NATO demonstrates that purchasing local goods and services has the potential to create an economic stimulus for Afghanistan.

4. Together, the expenditures of NATO and ISAF Contributing Nations in support of ISAF activities are significant. By reorienting resources towards the Afghan economy, ISAF has the potential to enhance Afghan economic development. While the top priority for all NATO procurement for operations is to ensure efficient, effective missions and the security of the civilian and military personnel, experiences demonstrate that making the maximum use of local goods and

services is advantageous for Afghanistan and ISAF Contributing Nations.

5. Procuring goods and services from Afghan companies promotes sustainable economic development by creating jobs, building economic capacities, developing the private and banking sectors, encouraging the development of infrastructure and generating tax revenue to support the delivery of services to the people of Afghanistan. Afghan firms know the market and can often provide quality goods and services at competitive prices. With a shorter supply chain, local procurement is often the best way for the buyer to maximize value and the timely delivery of needed goods and services. Increased local procurement allows local businesses to grow, gain experience, and generate jobs in the industrial,

commercial, service and agricultural sectors.

Procuring Afghan Goods and Services Using NATO Common Funds

6. The **Afghan First Policy** and the proposed practical steps, set out below, are aimed at strengthening NATO's contribution to the economic development of Afghanistan and provides for fair and equal opportunities for Afghan companies and employees through the following measures:

6.1. Allowing for Afghan participation in the NATO procurement process, wherever possible, without requiring ad hoc decisions on waivers.

6.2. Increasing local procurement of goods and services that originate in

Afghanistan whenever the acceptable standards for security, quality, price and reliable supply are met; making a clear preference in statements of work for local Afghan content, including the use of Afghan contractors and the employment of Afghan labour for works and jobs in Afghanistan.

6.3. Local procurement should not be hindered by procedural obstacles, but should be actively encouraged at all levels. All relevant stakeholders and NATO bodies are encouraged to consider adjustments to their practices according to the following practical recommendations to maximise, to the extent possible, the positive impact of NATO/ISAF presence and support the development of the Afghan economy.

6.4. Supporting local businesses by taking into consideration the specific requirements of Afghan companies and facilitating, to the extent possible, the participation of local Afghan businesses in competition for NATO procurement contracts, taking into account value for money.

6.5. In order to achieve a clearer picture on local procurement, develop reporting procedures regarding the number and value of contracts with local companies; prime contractors should be contractually obliged to report on local procurement of goods and services as well as subcontracting to local companies.

7. In addition, a number of practical steps will need to be taken to further facilitate Afghan participation in local procurement. These include:

7.1. improving pre-deployment preparations for personnel responsible for contracting and procurement, including increasing information about the local marketplace and its capabilities;

7.2. seeking out qualified and capable Afghan firms and sharing information with other contracting authorities;

7.3. working with Afghan authorities to qualify local companies as technically, financially and professionally capable and certify their country of origin;

7.4. simplifying bidding and contracting documents, providing translations where necessary and reducing the size of contracts; 7.5. enhancing measures to reduce the risks of corruption; and

7.6. supporting the development of Afghan skills through promoting training and mentoring activities currently provided by the International Community to local companies and employees.